What People Are Saying...

Lisa Frederiksen's easy-to-understand review of new brain and addiction-related research provides the foundation for breaking the generation-to-generation cycle of substance abuse - knowledge. Her research explains how the cycle of addiction is perpetuated physiologically, not only in substance abusers themselves, but also in family members and friends. I have found this information to be invaluable in helping relieve my patients of the burdens and shame associated with life with a substance-abuser, empowering them to take control of their own lives—the first step in breaking this cycle. I am thrilled to recommend Lisa's latest book, Loved One in Treatment? Now What!

Cherie Zappas Tannenbaum, Nurse Practitioner

We may not want to admit it but alcoholism and drug addiction is a family disease and must be treated that way. As well, many treatment facilities do not address the family, only the addict. Loved One In Treatment? Now What!, *by Lisa Frederiksen, helps the family members understand the scientific, medical, emotional, and physical components of the chronic disease so that they can support the addict in the recovery process.*

Although this book is based on scientific and medical research, it is written in lay language that is easy to understand and absorb. As well, Frederiksen's writing has undertones of her talking directly to the reader with understanding and compassion while encouraging the family members to "look after themselves" emotionally, mentally, and physically. The information is well researched, concise, and cutting-edge. In all honesty, this book is much more than I can put into words to give it the justice it deserves.

Irene Watson, co-author of Rewriting Life Scripts:
Transformational Recovery for Families of Addicts,
and author of The Sitting Swing:
Finding Wisdom to Know the Difference

How does alcoholism/addiction actually imprint on the structures of the brain? What really happens to the brain of an alcoholic or addict? In Loved One In Treatment? Now What!, *Lisa Frederiksen tells you exactly what is going on and how it affects the behavior of a loved one who suffers from alcohol or drug abuse and/or addiction. In this excellent book, written for family members, Frederiksen does a masterful job in pointing out how they themselves are an essential part of the treatment plan for an alcoholic/addict loved one. Loaded with accurate technical and behavioral details, this new book is certainly a must-read for professionals in the field as well. Bravo!*

Judith L. London, Ph.D., Licensed Psychologist
and author of *Connecting the Dots:*
Breakthroughs in Communication
as Alzheimer's Advances

Clear, honest and uncomplicated.... Lisa Frederiksen takes her life under-standing of substance abuse and addiction and adds to it her years of research on addiction and the brain to provide insight and information everyone needs in order to understand the impact "second hand drinking/drugging" has on our families and culture. This is a must read for anyone working in the field of addiction and is a tremendous gift for families stepping into the world of recovery.

Karin Bloom, M.S., PPSC
Over 20 years experience counseling
children and their families.

This is a wonderful handbook for those with substance addicted family members, significant others, and friends. Certainly your addict needs help; but don't ever forget, you do, as well. And Lisa brings it to you with her usual thorough research and pleasant writing style. Truly a great read, and companion, that will very nicely pull you through some difficult times.

Bill White, M.S.
chipur.com
sharing, learning and relief for
depression, anxiety, and bipolar disorder

Loved One In Treatment? Now What!

An Essential Handbook for Family Members and
Friends Navigating the Path of a Loved One's Addiction,
Treatment and Recovery

By Lisa Frederiksen

REDWOOD CITY, CA
www.kljpublishing.com

KLJ Publishing
www.kljpublishing.com

Printed in the United States of America

ISBN: 978-0-9816844-5-1

Library of Congress Control Number: 2009905582

WARNING AND DISCLAIMER

Dedicated To

...the countless numbers of family members and friends affected by a loved one's substance misuse. It really can get better.

Table of Contents

Loved One In Treatment? Now What!

An Essential Handbook for Family Members and Friends Navigating the Path of a Loved One's Addiction, Treatment and Recovery

CHAPTER 1

Why you? What now?

Why?

Why you? Why *your* loved one? And, why read *this* particular book?

To answer the last question, I have been where you are now. I have more than forty years of experience with family alcohol abuse and alcoholism, including seven-plus years of research and recovery work unraveling the effects. I absolutely know the pain, confusion, anger, frustration, hope and despair you may be feeling at this time. I absolutely know it can and does get better. And I now have enough experience to know it gets better far more quickly when you understand the 21st century brain and addiction-related research, the impacts a loved one's substance abuse and/or addiction has on family members and friends and what you can do to help yourself as all of this unfolds.

After one of my loved ones entered treatment for alcoholism several years ago, I decided to use my resources as a researcher and author of six previously published books to write, *If You Loved Me, You'd Stop! What You Really Need To Know When Your Loved One Drinks Too Much*, in order to share these findings with others. I have since incorporated that research, and continuously update it, on my blog, www.breakingthecycles.com, and in my work as a consultant and speaker on issues related to alcohol and addiction.

The groups and individuals I work with are varied and vast. They include medical school students, treatment center clients and their families, troops and military personnel, teachers and parents, middle school students, domestic violence professionals, family law attorneys, clinicians, college students and community organizations. I share this research as a guest on radio, television and internet programs, and it forms the basis of the courses I teach as an approved substance abuse/mental illness MCLE provider (continuing legal education training) for the California Bar Association.

As For This Particular Book…

Loved One In Treatment? Now What! is the culmination of all these experiences. It is written to help you – the family member or friend – answer the scores of questions you likely have, such as:

How can it be a disease when they *choose* to drink or use? Why isn't there a straightforward answer for what's going on? Why don't I feel better now that my loved one has decided to get (or at least seems open to getting) treatment for an addiction to alcohol and/or drugs? I should be thrilled – happy!

Instead, you likely feel scared, confused, angry, sad, numb, resigned, fed-up or desperate. You may be stunned and confused or believe you are a bad parent, sibling, friend or spouse because you were not even aware your loved one was abusing drugs or alcohol. You may find your feelings are entirely different from those of another family member or friend, which can bring you back to the question, "Why?"

And now you find yourself faced with a whole new world – the "world" of addiction treatment and recovery – one that includes concepts and programs, such as Alcoholics Anonymous (AA), Narcotics Anonymous (NA), detox, residential in-patient, intensive outpatient, family therapy, dual diagnosis, continuing care, drug testing, medications for cravings, denial, Al-Anon or Nar-Anon. And all of this brings up even more questions:

What is an addiction? How is it even possible? And, what do you mean, "I'm a codependent; an enabler?"

"Why?"

Secrecy and Shame

When Robert Smith and Bill Wilson (Dr. Bob and Bill W.) co-founded Alcoholics Anonymous (AA) in 1935, the concept of alcoholism as an illness began to take hold in the United States. It would be decades before a similar view of drug addiction surfaced.

Prior to 1935, much of society viewed individuals who had a problem with their drinking as weak-willed. People believed *those* individuals lacked the moral fortitude and willpower to get their drinking under control. They believed *those* people consciously chose to drink, in spite of the physical, emotional or financial costs to their families and friends.

Those beliefs caused "treatment" to consist primarily of a stay in a sanitarium and/or efforts to make the person drink less – not to abstain entirely but to drink less; to get it under control. And as far as society was concerned, it was up to the family and friends to make that happen if the "drinker" could not. It was up to the family members and friends to keep it under wraps and to cover-up the fall out, such as making excuses to the boss for a loved one's absence from work – again.

And when the family member or friend could not reform the drinker or hush up the problem, they felt shame of their own; shame for not being important enough for their loved one to want to stop. This shame often turned into anger, sadness and hopelessness as family members and friends made one failed attempt after another to get loved ones to change their drinking patterns.

Struggling to control the perceived cause – alcohol – led American citizens to rally behind the Temperance Movement in the 1800s. Eventually, the movement convinced a nation that ridding society of alcohol would rid society of drunkenness. And so the United States ratified the 18th Amendment to its Constitution in 1919, making it illegal to sell, manufacture or transport alcohol.

It was known as Prohibition, but infringing on a person's rights with regards to alcohol did not go over well in a country that prides itself on the rights to free speech and to bear arms. Fourteen years later Prohibition was overturned, but the fall-out continues today. Much of society still views public attempts to talk about problems related to alcohol as "code" for wanting to take away a person's right to drink in whatever manner they so choose to drink.

Recovering in Anonymity Continues the Secrecy and Shame

The founding of AA provided the first wide-spread effort to view excessive drinking as something beyond a "lack of willpower" and to approach treatment from the perspective of abstinence – not drinking *any* alcohol. Its fellowship viewed alcoholism as a "combination of physical, psychological and spiritual causes," a combination that made alcoholics *different* from non-alcoholics.

AA provided a guide for how a member of its fellowship could achieve abstinence and a joyful life through its 12-steps and *The Big Book*. It proved to be life-changing then and continues to be life-changing now for millions who grapple with alcoholism – today understood as one of the diseases of addiction. However, AA could not overcome the shame in which society had so thoroughly shrouded the problem, a shame so powerful it forced alcoholics to recover from their disease in anonymity, hence the name, Alcoholics Anonymous.

Treatment options for drug addictions took even longer. Narcotics Anonymous (NA) meetings patterned after AA did not appear until the early 1950s, and its guidebook, *Basic Text*, was published long after that.

Not until the early 1980s, with the co-founding of the Betty Ford Clinic by Former First Lady Betty Ford, did seeking treatment at a residential facility for alcohol and drug addictions gain public recognition. Today, there are more than 11,000 addiction treatment programs in the United States, according to the U.S. Department of Health and Human Services, Substance Abuse and Mental Health Awareness Services (SAMHAS). And organizations, such as the American Medical Association, the National Institute on Drug Abuse, the World Health Organization and the National Institute on Alcohol Abuse and Alcoholism, are making significant advances in the prevention and treatment of alcoholism and drug addiction.

Yet, these major inroads have not been enough to overcome the secrecy and shame in which society has so thoroughly encased the problem. As a consequence, alcoholism and drug addiction continue to be misunderstood diseases. They continue to be diseases people try to conquer on their own or to recover from in anonymity for fear of the reprisals they may face socially, at school, in the workplace or within their extended families.

In 2010, people still try to recover in anonymity. But new brain and addiction-related research is exploding our long-held beliefs about alcoholism and drug addiction being a matter of "choice." Finally we can end the secrecy and shame!

Very Little in the Way of Help for Family Members and Friends

And through it all, there is and has been very little to specifically help the family members and friends – the people so deeply affected by a loved one's substance abuse and/or addiction. Yes, there is Al-Anon, a 12-step program co-founded by Lois Wilson, the wife of AA co-founder, Bill W., for anyone whose life has been affected by a loved one's alcohol misuse. And there is Nar-Anon, a similar program for family members and friends of drug addicts or drug abusers. Both have been lifelines for millions. And, yes, many treatment centers offer a family program of some kind. But overall, there has been relatively little focus on understanding and treating the many effects of *secondhand drinking/drugging*.

Secondhand drinking/drugging (SHDD) is a term used to describe the impacts of a person's alcohol or drug misuse on others. These impacts are significant – profoundly significant. They are the fall-out – the being on the receiving end of the nasty, mean, hurtful exchanges that occur during fights about the substance misuse... the DUIs... the arrests... the binge drinking... the blackouts... the unprotected or unwanted sex... the verbal, emotional or physical abuse... the broken promises...you know your list. These behaviors are called substance misuse behaviors.

Secondhand drinking/drugging impacts are the consequences of a spouse, parent, child or sibling trying to pick up the pieces by cowering, placating, hiding to stay safe, excusing, regrouping, pleading, protecting the children, bartering and finally steeling him/herself for the next time their loved one abuses their substance of choice. The ways in which secondhand drinking/drugging affects family members and friends, include: worry and/or anxiety, fear, isolation, anger, frustration, low self-esteem and health problems. These impacts can also contribute to a person's risk factors for developing substance abuse problems and/or the disease of addiction.

> *Secondhand drinking/ drugging can have profound, lasting effects on family members and friends – very much the same way secondhand smoke affects the health of those living within the close sphere of the smoker.*

Helping Family Members and Friends Needs To Be On Par With Helping Addicts and Alcoholics

By the time treatment is sought or acknowledged as necessary, family members and friends have generally been living with secondhand drinking/drugging for some time. That's because addiction does not just strike one day – like waking up with the flu. Instead, it slowly creeps forward as a person's substance use moves from the occasional to abuse to dependence (a.k.a. addiction). This means all concerned – the person with the addiction and those who love him or her – have been at this for a long time; in some cases, a very long time.

This constant conflict over the behaviors that accompany substance misuse can leave family members and friends feeling a range of emotions – anger, hatred, helplessness, sadness, fear…. As a result, when their loved one finally begins or seriously considers treatment, it can be overwhelming – especially when the family member or friend does not know what to expect from a treatment program and learns there is no clear, short answer to the question, "Now what?"

Instead, the focus is once again on the addict or alcoholic, which is a focus family members and friends have been party to for far too long. They want and need help; they want and need answers, and that is where this book comes in.

One 10-year old girl explained how she could tell if her mom was drunk by the droop of her eyelids. On one particular occasion, the girl assured her friend, who was worried about the way the girl's mom was "acting" and "talking kind of funny," that it was okay to ride in the car with her mom driving because her mom's eyes weren't "too closed." On that drive, the mom got into a car accident and killed one of the other girls in the car. The mom's BAC (blood alcohol content) was .132.

About This Book

Purposefully short, this book is written for family members and friends of a loved one with an addiction to alcohol or illegal or prescription drugs and for anyone interested in learning about the new science behind addiction, addiction treatment and the impact of secondhand drinking/drugging on families, friends and communities. It will help readers understand:

- the new brain research that is providing the science-based answers to the questions, "Why is addiction a disease?" "Why does my loved one have it and not 'so-in-so' (someone else), who drinks far more?"
- how the science of brain development and brain functioning can help with treatment of and recovery from an addiction
- what coping with the impacts of secondhand drinking/drugging does to family members and friends and what they can do to help themselves (and in that process, help their loved one).

This book will also help readers learn:

- what treatment can do
- how to talk to friends, extended family and children about a loved one's addiction
- how to "talk" to an addicted loved one so that effective communication can be established
- what family members and friends can and cannot do to help a loved one's recovery

- what all concerned can expect in the years ahead.

Overall, the first half of the book is to help you understand the disease of addiction. The second half is to help you understand how a loved one's addiction affects you and what you can do to help yourself.

The following checklist lays out a guide for "next steps." The remainder of the book provides the information you will need to check the items off the list. Consider it a road map, if you will; an answer to your overriding question, "Now what?"

As you read through this checklist, don't let your immediate reaction to one or more of the statements stop you. For example, the statement calling addiction a disease might cause some readers to think, "Like *!?!#* it is!" and toss the book aside. But, as you will learn in Chapter 3, this research is new – much of it published in just the past decade. So it will be important to keep an open mind until you make it all the way through the book.

"I could tell it was going to be a bad night," one wife explained. "He called me at 10:00, long after the kids and I had gone to bed, telling me he was on his way. He wanted me to thaw a steak so he could barbeque it. When I refused, he made as much noise as he could when he got home, slamming every cupboard door. I didn't make a sound, praying he wouldn't come into our bedroom. Around 1:00 a.m., I found him passed out at the barbeque. The steak was burnt to a crisp.

Checklist of Next Steps for Family Members and Friends of an Addict or Alcoholic in (or Seriously Considering) Treatment

____ **Conduct an informal assessment** to determine if your loved one's drug or alcohol use pattern follows that of an addict/alcoholic, Chapter 2.

____ **Learn about the explosion in brain research** during the past 15-20 years, Chapter 3.

____ **Learn how the new brain research and study findings** are revolutionizing our understanding of addiction, Chapters 4 and 5.

____ **Learn about the disease of addiction,** whether it be an addiction to drugs or alcohol, Chapter 6.

____ **Accept your loved one has the disease of addiction (if they do),** Chapter 7.

____ **Learn what to look for in and expect from addiction treatment and recovery,** Chapter 8.

____ **Learn what's happened to you** – that is, understand the effects of secondhand drinking/drugging, Chapter 9.

____ **Understand the connection between secondhand drinking/ drugging and codependency,** Chapter 10.

____ **Understand key concepts to start taking control of your life,** Chapter 11.

____ **Learn about the additional tools that can help *you* whether or not your loved one starts and/or continues treatment and recovery,** Chapter 12

____ **Learn why family members and friends may perceive the situation differently and how to talk** to your children, extended family and friends about what is going on, Chapter 13.

Key Terms Going Forward

You will hear many new terms relative to your loved one's treatment and recovery. The following explanations will help you start to understand this new world you have been thrown into. As you continue reading, other terms will also be defined.

Addiction – whether it's an addiction to alcohol or illegal or prescription drugs, collectively referred to as "drugs," "addiction is a chronic, often relapsing brain disease that causes compulsive drug seeking and use despite harmful consequences to the individual who is addicted and to those around them."[1]

Alcoholic – identifies a person addicted to alcohol (a person who has the disease of alcoholism).

Alcohol and illegal and prescription drugs are all considered "drugs." (NIDA)

Codependent – a term often assigned to the family member or friend of an alcoholic or drug addict. It is a complicated concept to explain without first having an understanding of the disease of addiction. So for now, it just helps to know the term and know it is fully explained in Chapter 10.

Drug Addict – the common term used to identify a person addicted to an illegal and/or prescription drug. The term is often shortened to "addict."

Secondhand drinking/drugging (SHDD) – describes the impacts of a person's substance abuse or addiction on others – especially on family members and friends, but also on co-workers, fellow students and communities-at-large. The term is meant to cause impressions similar to those a person has when they hear the words, "secondhand smoke," a term that immediately brings to mind the impacts of a person's smoking on others.

Substance Abuse – the term used to describe drinking or using more of a drug or alcohol than the brain or body can process and as a result, engaging in substance misuse behaviors. Common variations of this term include alcohol abuse and drug abuse. Repeated substance abuse causes chemical and structural changes in the brain. These brain changes contribute to a person developing the disease of addiction. Substance abuse also causes secondhand drinking/drugging impacts, as does addiction.

Substance Misuse – includes both substance abuse and addiction because both cause a person to engage in substance misuse behaviors. It is the substance misuse behaviors, regardless of the label, that cause the problems for the substance abuser, addict/alcoholic, family, friends and communities-at-large.

Substance Misuse Behaviors – describes the behaviors a person engages in when they drink or use more drugs than their body and brain can process. These include arguments about the drinking, getting into fights, driving while under the influence (DUI), doing poorly in school or at work because of the substance misuse or having to recover from the misuse, having unwanted or unprotected or unplanned sex, binge drinking (defined as four or more standard drinks on a single occasion for women and five or more standard drinks on a single occasion for men) or blacking out.

12-step program. This term refers to several programs, all based on the 12-steps of Alcoholics Anonymous (AA). Two are NA (Narcotics Anonymous) and AA (Alcoholics Anonymous), which are for persons addicted to illegal or prescription drugs (NA) or alcohol (AA). Three additional 12-step programs referenced in addiction recovery circles are for the families and friends of an addict/alcoholic. They are Nar-Anon (drugs), Al-Anon (alcohol – adults) and Alateen (alcohol – young people, 13 and up). There are others, as well. Each has a website where you can find meeting times and locations.

Treatment. There are many treatment options because no one person's recovery will follow a path identical to another's, but regardless of the options used, effective addiction treatment should follow a disease management approach and include: 1) detox/stabilization, 2) rehabilitation (rehab) and 3) continuing care. Often, people engage in a combination of treatment options, which may include cognitive behavioral therapy (CBT), medications, a 12-step program, mindfulness programs (for example, yoga), spiritual and/or religious programs or activities, healthy nutrition, exercise, group meetings, counseling, intensive outpatient (the person does not live at the treatment center but attends treatment programs at the center during the day and/or evening), residential treatment (the person lives at the treatment center) and continuing care (a plan for what to do after rehab [rehabilitation]). Chapter 8 explains treatment and recovery in more detail.

All of the above terms and concepts will become clearer as you continue reading.

CHAPTER 2

Is It Really Alcoholism?
Is It Really a Drug Addiction?

Likely, you have been trying for years to get your loved one to stop drinking and/or using drugs. Your efforts probably seemed to work – at least sometimes.

You probably experienced periods when your loved one did stop or cut down or changed or cleaned up. But then something would happen, and it would start again, and you would rev up your efforts to make it stop. These efforts may have included:

- loaning him money to set up an apartment or buy a car or start school or tide him over until he got that new job

- letting her live with you without contributing much financially to household bills or chores because she had nowhere else to go

- deciding to "just do it myself" when confronted with laundry or children's needs or household chores left undone because she wasn't feeling well or had been "out"

- believing his lies or coming up with your own rationalizations for how the lies could possibly be true because the truth was incomprehensible.

It is possible you are not entirely convinced – even now – that your loved one is an alcoholic or a drug addict, especially if s/he is a young person.

It is no wonder, really. People who have a problem with their substance use often try to minimize how bad it, often comparing their use to someone else's and making statements like, "I'm not as bad as Joe. Heck, he drinks every day!"

Family members often offer similar rationalizations because they can't believe their loved one is an alcoholic or drug addict. They think of alcoholics and addicts as older or homeless or without jobs or families – conditions that do not apply to their loved ones.

Additionally, despite the progress made since the time of Betty Ford's treatment, much of society still views alcoholism and drug addiction as conditions caused by an individual's lack of willpower. This stigma makes it nearly impossible to talk productively about the drinking/drugging behaviors with a loved one, within a family or with close friends, let alone with a doctor, teacher or boss. To have such an honest conversation might mean we believe our loved one is an addict/alcoholic. And that would be bad, bad, bad. What would people think? What would the boss say? What would that even mean? And so it continues. Family members, friends and the loved one with the substance misuse problem trudge on in isolation making one failed attempt after another to make it all stop.

Conducting your own informal assessment can help you understand your loved one's substance abuse patterns and where those patterns fit with regards to addiction.

For these reasons, it can be helpful to complete an informal assessment of your loved one's alcohol or drug use in order to verify what it is you are actually dealing with. To that end, you should complete one of the following assessments (the first is for alcohol, the second is for drugs) as if you are your loved one "talking." In other words, you will answer the questions based on your understanding of your loved one's substance abuse patterns and behaviors.

Completing one (or both) of these assessment does NOT constitute a formal diagnosis. That is done by a clinician working with your loved one or by your loved one's own admission. But, honestly assessing the situation will help you let go of fighting with your loved one and/or fighting your own thoughts and feelings about the situation. It will enable you to be more open to what you need to do for yourself as you continue reading – namely, learn about the disease of addiction and why it happens to some and not to others and recognize what living with it has done to you.

AUDIT = Alcohol Use Assessment

DAST = Drug Use Assessment

Assessing Your Loved One's _Alcohol_ Use

The following assessment was developed and evaluated over a period of two decades by the World Health Organization's (WHO) Department of Mental Health and Substance Dependence. It is called AUDIT (the Alcohol Use Disorders

Identification Test). It was created primarily for health care practitioners around the world as a simple method of screening for excessive drinking.[2]

Note: as you complete the assessment, don't forget that the "size" of a drink matters. 1.5 ounces of 80-proof liquor, 5 ounces of wine and 12 ounces of regular beer all equal ONE standard drink. Sometimes it's helpful to actually measure and pour these quantities into your commonly used glasses in order to "see" what a standard drink of a particular type of alcohol actually looks like.

Illustration 2.1 Visual of "A" Standard Drink of Various Alcoholic Beverages

L to R: 5 ounces of wine, 1.5 ounces of bourbon, 1.5 ounce shot of vodka, 1.5 ounces of vodka on–the–rocks, 3.3 ounces of champagne, 12 ounces of regular beer. Each drink pictured contains the same amount of alcohol, although liquid amounts vary considerably. Courtesy Jessica Scott

Also, it's important to understand that all types of people and establishments (including bars, restaurants, alcoholics, alcohol abusers, neighbors and friends), pour "drinks" which actually contain more alcohol than the amount defined as one "Standard Drink." A margarita, for example, often contains two to three standard drinks.

And, now for the assessment. Circle the answer that best applies to your perception of your loved one's drinking. In other words, answer as though your loved one is taking the assessment.

1. How often do you have a drink containing alcohol?
   (0) Never
   (1) Monthly or less
   (2) 2 to 4 times a month
   (3) 2 to 3 times a week
   (4) 4 or more times a week

2. How many drinks containing alcohol do you have on a typical day when you are drinking?

   (0) 1 or 2
   (1) 3 or 4
   (2) 5 or 6
   (3) 7, 8, or 9
   (4) 10 or more

3. How often do you have six or more drinks on one occasion [note: this is known as binge drinking, and in the U.S., binge drinking is five or more drinks on one occasion for men and four or more drinks on one occasion for women]?

   (0) Never
   (1) Less than monthly
   (2) Monthly
   (3) Weekly
   (4) Daily or almost daily

4. How often during the last year have you found that you were not able to stop drinking once you had started?

   (0) Never
   (1) Less than monthly
   (2) Monthly
   (3) Weekly
   (4) Daily or almost daily

5. How often during the last year have you failed to do what was normally expected from you because of drinking?

   (0) Never
   (1) Less than monthly
   (2) Monthly
   (3) Weekly
   (4) Daily or almost daily

6. How often during the last year have you needed a first drink in the morning to get yourself going after a heavy drinking session?

   (0) Never
   (1) Less than monthly
   (2) Monthly
   (3) Weekly
   (4) Daily or almost daily

7. How often during the last year have you had a feeling of guilt or remorse after drinking?

    (0) Never

    (1) Less than monthly

    (2) Monthly

    (3) Weekly

    (4) Daily or almost daily

8. How often during the last year have you been unable to remember what happened the night before because you had been drinking?

    (0) Never

    (1) Less than monthly

    (2) Monthly

    (3) Weekly

    (4) Daily or almost daily

9. Have you or someone else been injured as a result of your drinking?

    (0) No

    (2) Yes, but not in the last year

    (4) Yes, during the last year

10. Has a relative or friend or a doctor or another health worker been concerned about your drinking or suggested you cut down?

    (0) No

    (2) Yes, but not in the last year

    (4) Yes, during the last year

Now, look at the numbers in the parentheses ( ) for each answer you've circled and add them up. According to AUDIT, total scores between 8 and 19 indicate alcohol abuse (excessive drinking). Total scores 20 and above indicate alcohol dependence (alcoholism).[3] A score of 0-7 indicates drinking at moderate levels. This is also known as "normal" drinking or "alcohol use."

Caution: The AUDIT goes on to say that in the absence of a trained professional administering this assessment (as he or she knows how to ask the question and interpret the answer or dig more deeply for an accurate answer), these guidelines and scoring must be considered tentative – NOT definitive. Additionally, the AUDIT notes that in an "official" evaluation, the questions on which points were scored matters. So it's important to review the entire AUDIT document and not to draw any firm conclusions, leaving that to a professional treatment team or to your loved one's own admission.

When you have completed the AUDIT, stop and take a breath. Now you know. Your loved one has a problem. Perhaps you've always known, but now you can see it in black and white. Or perhaps you may be one of the fortunate few to discover your loved one's problem is not as bad as you feared. In either case, you should give yourself a little time to let the results of the AUDIT sink in. Once you have done that, you'll be in a better position to appreciate the differences between alcohol use, abuse and dependence as explained next.

Three Stages of Drinking – Use, Abuse, Dependence (a.k.a. Alcoholism)

For most of us, we think of drinking as either "normal" or "alcoholic." For this reason, people often go to great lengths to prove they are not an alcoholic or to avoid calling a loved one an alcoholic. This can cause a person to abuse alcohol or to tolerate the substance misuse behaviors of someone who does, which is how the problems all start.

"I mean," one wife said, "he goes to work everyday. He's not mean to me or our daughters. I mean, yeah, sure he got a DUI and I can't get him up off the couch most Saturday nights, but there's no way he's an alcoholic."

Alcohol "use" is defined as "normal" or "moderate" drinking limits. The idea is that if a person stays within these limits, 1) s/he will not drink more than their brains and body can process [a.k.a. binge drinking], and therefore they will stay in control of their thinking and their behaviors, and 2) his/her alcohol consumption will not get in the way of their overall health [each drink contains about 100 calories and very few nutrients, for example].

Moderate drinking limits are defined by the National Institute on Alcohol Abuse and Alcoholism (NIAAA) as:

No more than 7 standard drinks per week, nor 3 of those 7 in one day, for women.

No more than 14 standard drinks per week, nor 4 of those 14 in one day, for men.

Part of this definition is to understand that a standard drink is either 5 ounces of table wine, 12 ounces of regular beer or 1.5 ounces of hard liquor (i.e., vodka). Many cocktails contain more than one Standard Drink.

Alcohol abuse is when a person repeatedly drinks more than moderate limits and engages in the substance misuse behaviors described below. The American Psychiatric Association's Diagnostic and Statistical Manual of Mental Disorders, Fourth Edition (DSM-IV), defines the criteria for alcohol abuse as:

1. *A maladaptive pattern of alcohol abuse leading to clinically significant impairment or distress, as manifested by* one or more *of the following,* occurring within a 12-month period (emphasis added):

   - *Recurrent alcohol use resulting in failure to fulfill major role obligations at work, school, or home (e.g., repeated absences or poor work performance related to substance use; substance-related absences, suspensions or expulsions from school; or neglect of children or household).*

- Recurrent alcohol use in situations in which it is physically hazardous (e.g., driving an automobile or operating a machine).

- Recurrent alcohol-related legal problems (e.g., arrests for alcohol-related disorderly conduct).

- Continued alcohol use despite persistent or recurrent social or interpersonal problems caused or exacerbated by the effects of the alcohol

"Mommy and her friends always drink their wine out of pretty glasses while we play. They say they're having a 'mommy play date,'" said one child. "But sometimes she doesn't act like my mommy."

(e.g., arguments with spouse about consequences of intoxication or physical fights).

2. *These symptoms must never have met the criteria for alcohol dependence* [meaning a person's symptoms do not meet those for a diagnosis of alcohol dependence].

Alcohol abuse is the stage during which the secondhand drinking impacts for family members and friends begin. Repeated alcohol abuse causes chemical and structural changes in the brain like those shown in Chapter 3, Image 3.1.

Alcohol dependence (a.k.a. an addiction to alcohol, a.k.a. alcoholism) is one of the diseases of addiction (fully described in Chapter 6).

The label doesn't matter. Both alcohol abuse and alcoholism cause secondhand drinking impacts for family members and friends.

Throwing Up Does Not Get Rid of the Alcohol... neither does a walk, drinking coffee, exercising or taking a cold shower. The only thing that can sober a person up is time. Understanding the concepts presented in this sidebar can help explain why your loved one behaved the way s/he did given the quantities of alcohol consumed.

Alcohol enters the bloodstream through the walls of the small intestine. Because alcohol dissolves in water, the bloodstream carries it throughout the body (which is 60-70% water) where it is absorbed into body tissue in proportion to the body tissue's water content. The alcohol then "sits" in the tissues until it is broken down (metabolized) by the liver. The brain, heart and liver are especially affected by repeated alcohol abuse and/or alcoholism.

It takes specific enzymes produced in the liver an AVERAGE of 1 hour to metabolize 1 standard drink; 4 hours to metabolize 4 drinks – even if the drinks were consumed back-to-back, and it's been over an hour since the last drink.

Since the brain is mostly water, alcohol "sits" in the brain until it is metabolized, suppressing certain brain functions, which is why a person who drinks more than their liver can process finds him/herself engaging in drinking behaviors (a.k.a. substance misuse behaviors).

Assessing Your Loved One's Legal or Illegal Drug Use

The previous AUDIT evaluation was designed to assess your loved one's use and behaviors surrounding alcohol. But perhaps you are more concerned about your loved one's use or abuse of drugs (whether legal or illegal). In that case, you should complete the assessment which follows. This adapted assessment is based on the Drug Abuse Screening Test (DAST), which was developed by HA Skinner as a brief instrument for clinical screening and treatment evaluation research. The full DAST can be found in Join Together's booklet, *Screening & Brief Intervention: Making a Public Health Difference.*[4] (Join Together is a project of the Boston University School of Public Health and supports community-based efforts to advance effective alcohol and drug policy, prevention, and treatment.)

Please answer Y or N to the following questions as if the question was directed to your loved one. In other words, answer as though your loved one is describing his or her use and behaviors over the past 12 months.

1. Have you used drugs other than those required for medical reasons?
   __ Y __ N

2. Have you abused prescription drugs [taken more than prescribed by your doctor]?   __ Y __ N

3. Do you abuse more than one drug at a time?   __ Y __ N

4. Are you unable to get through the week without using drugs?
   __ Y __ N

5. Are you unable to stop using drugs when you want to?   __ Y __ N

6. Have you had "blackouts" or "flashbacks" as a result of drug use?
   __ Y __ N

7. Do you ever feel bad or guilty about your drug use?   __ Y __ N

8. Does your spouse (or parents) ever complain about your involvement with drugs?   __ Y __ N

9. Has drug abuse created problems between you and your spouse or your parents?   __ Y __ N

10. Have you lost friends because of your use of drugs?   __ Y __ N

11. Have you neglected your family because of your use of drugs?
    __ Y __ N

12. Have you been in trouble at work because of your use of drugs?
    __ Y __ N

13. Have you lost a job because of drug abuse?   __ Y __ N

14. Have you gotten into fights or been arrested for a DUI or unusual behaviors when under the influence of drugs? __ Y __ N

15. Have you engaged in illegal activities in order to obtain drugs?
    __ Y __ N

16. Have you been arrested for possession of illegal drugs? __ Y __ N

17. Have you ever experienced withdrawal symptoms (felt sick) when you stopped taking drugs?   __ Y __ N

18. Have you had medical problems as a result of your drug use (e.g., memory loss, hepatitis, convulsions, bleeding, etc.)?
    __ Y __ N

19. Have you gone to anyone for help for a drug problem? __ Y __ N

20. Have you been involved in a treatment program especially related to drug use?   __ Y __ N

Now add up the total number of YES answers. A score of 4 or more YES answers indicates a possible problem of drug abuse or drug dependence. Again, as with the alcohol use assessment, this is not to be construed as an official diagnosis; that is something determined by a professional treatment team or your loved one's admission. But it may help you in the beginning to recognize and understand the scope of the problem you've been facing.

So if it's this easy to determine, why has it been so hard? Why don't doctors identify it early on? Why does everyone act as if it's not real?

Why? Because most people do not know of or understand the new brain research and the new science-based answers that are now unraveling the mysteries of addiction. But you will begin to understand both as you continue reading the next several chapters.

Co-Addictions

A high score on both the AUDIT and the DAST indicates a co-addiction. This means, your loved one could be addicted to two or more substances at the same time. It is also not uncommon to have a substance addiction occurring at the same time as another addition, such as gambling.

Checking items off the list...

(Refer to Chapter 1 for the full "Checklist of Next Steps for Family Members and Friends of an Addict or Alcoholic in [or Seriously Considering] Treatment")

✔ **Conduct an informal assessment to determine if your loved one's drug or alcohol use pattern follows that of an addict/alcoholic.**

Points to Remember:

- The size of a "drink" can vary widely from place to place, which means that when loved ones say they've "only had a couple," they could have consumed far more alcohol than they (or you) realize.

- Alcohol use, abuse and dependence (alcoholism) are three distinct phases but destructive behaviors can accompany both alcohol abuse and dependence.

- Completing an informal assessment using the AUDIT or DAST can help you clarify whether your loved one's drug or alcohol use pattern follows that of an addict/alcoholic.

- A loved one may be addicted to both alcohol and a drug, so he or she will need treatment for a co-addiction.

CHAPTER 3

What the New Brain Research Reveals About Addiction

We must thank two decades for the research findings that are exploding centuries-old beliefs about people who abuse substances – the 1990s, the "Decade of the Brain," and the 2000s, the "Decade of Discovery." These two decades unleashed unprecedented funding and collaborative efforts among neuroscientists and medical professionals, federal and private agencies, companies and foundations to study and understand the live human brain like never before.

The magnitude of what has been discovered is staggering. It is similar to the brilliant discoveries America and the world experienced as a result of President Kennedy's challenge in 1960 to put a man on the moon and bring him back to earth before the end of that decade. Scientists,

> *The "Decade of the Brain" (the 1990s) and the "Decade of Discovery" (the 2000s) have done for brain research what the decade of the 1960s did for space exploration.*

mathematicians, electrical engineers, astronauts, communication specialists, computer technology gurus, government agencies and the like met the President's challenge. And the world sat riveted to its televisions and radios on July 20, 1969, as astronauts Buzz Aldrin and Neil Armstrong planted the U.S. flag on the moon, and Armstrong proclaimed, "One small step for a man; one giant step for mankind."

That is what the decades of the 1990s and 2000s have done for our understanding of the brain, and from there, our understanding of the impact of alcohol and drugs on the brain.

New Brain Imaging Technologies

SPECT, MRI, and PET are examples of the imaging technologies that emerged during the Decade of the Brain. Because of these kinds of imagining technologies, science is no longer restricted to studying the brain through anatomical scans, such as CAT scans or MRIs, or post-mortem dissection. Instead, neuroscientists and medical professionals can view three dimensional images of the live human brain in action, giving them the capability to answer questions, like:

- how the brain works

- how it develops

- how it wires (via neural networks) and controls everything we think, do, say and feel
- how outside influences and genetics impact that wiring
- how a person can "rewire their brains" and thereby change their behaviors
- how substances, such as alcohol or drugs, impact the brain's neural networks and can actually change the chemical and structural make-up of the brain when repeatedly abused.

Advances in brain imaging technologies now allow scientists to study the LIVE human brain. This ability has resulted in huge advances in our understanding of how the brain develops and why abusing substances (drugs or alcohol) causes chemical and structural changes in the brain.

Image 3.1 (next page) provides an example of what can now be seen with the new imaging technologies. In this case, the technology is known as SPECT. SPECT stands for Single Photon Emission Computed Tomography. Dr. Daniel Amen, nationally-known author of *Change Your Brain, Change Your Body,* explains on the Amen Clinics website that SPECT "is a nuclear medicine study that uses radioisotopes as tracking devices to look at living brain tissue. The radiation exposure from one SPECT is one-third the level of radiation from an abdominal CAT scan, a very common procedure in medicine. SPECT gives a three dimensional view of brain activity. Basically, SPECT measures areas of the brain that work well, areas that are low in activity and areas that are high activity."[5]

Image 3.1 shows a comparison of a healthy brain (single image on left) vs. the brain of a man who drank three to four drinks a day following his daughter's departure for college (4 images on right). In other words, his wasn't a lifelong drinking pattern nor was he diagnosed as an alcoholic.

For comparison, look at the single image on the left and compare it to the bottom right image of the four scan series. These are both top-down scans of the brain. These scans are courtesy of the Amen Clinics, Inc., and can be viewed in color by visiting their website, www.amenclinics.com. You will also find similar scans on their website showing the effects of various types of drug abuse on the brain. Please note that these kinds of scans confirm the findings of a clinical diagnosis/evaluation; they are not diagnostic in and of themselves.

In Image 3.1, you will see what appear to be holes or bumps in the four images on the right. These are not actually holes, as in destroyed brain matter, rather they are areas of low blood flow and therefore areas of low brain activity. Of course you cannot understand the implications of these images at this point, but seeing them can help you better understand that "something" (more fully explained later in this chapter) definitely happens in the brain when a person abuses a substance (in this case alcohol). These images can also help you appreciate that this "something" likely has an impact on a person's ability to think straight and act responsibly.

What Alcohol Abuse
Does to the Brain

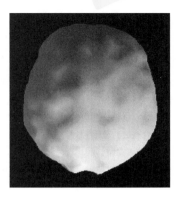

SPECT Surface Scan of Normal Brain

SPECT Surface Scans of 56 year old brain with
daily use - 3-4 drinks/day - but NOT an alcoholic

**Image 3.1 What Alcohol Abuse Does to the Brain
SPECT Surface Scans Courtesy of Amen Clinics, Inc., www.amenclinics.com**

A Whole New Understanding of Addiction Emerges

With these new brain imaging capabilities, there has been an explosion of research findings – many in just the past ten years, which is why the first decade of the 21st century is known as the "Decade of Discovery." What neuroscientists and medical professionals are learning is upending long-held beliefs about substance abuse, addiction and addiction treatment methods,[6] as well as the effects of secondhand drinking/drugging on family members and friends – especially the impact on *their* brains.

Perhaps the most important outcome for family members and friends and addicts/alcoholics is the emergence – finally – of a clear, scientifically-based definition of addiction as a brain disease. Whether it's an addiction to alcohol or drugs (illegal or prescription), the National Institute on Drug Abuse (NIDA) defines addiction as:

a chronic, often relapsing brain disease that causes compulsive drug seeking and use despite harmful consequences to the individual who is addicted and to those around them.

Addiction is a brain disease because the abuse of alcohol or drugs leads to changes in the structure and function of the brain. Although it is true that for most people the initial decision to take drugs or drink alcohol is voluntary, over time the changes in the brain caused by repeated drug or alcohol abuse can affect a person's self control and ability to make sound decisions, and at the same time send intense impulses to take the drugs or drink alcohol.

It is because of these changes in the brain that it is so challenging for a person who is addicted to stop abusing drugs or alcohol. Fortunately, there are treatments that help people to counteract addiction's powerful disruptive effects and regain control.[7]

So, if some of the best minds and leading researchers have concluded that addiction is a brain disease, why doesn't everybody know this?!

"Addiction is a brain disease." Just as people with heart disease have a condition that changes the normal functioning of their hearts, people with an addiction have a disease that changes the normal functioning of their brains.

The primary reason is the gap between the time when scientists make discoveries and the time when those discoveries become a part of common knowledge. For the general public, policy makers, medical schools, insurance companies, employers, teachers, and community leaders – even medical professionals – this research and these study findings are still very, very new. As such, much of this new research and its implications are not fully understood by doctors, clinicians, therapists, social workers, law enforcement officials and insurance underwriters – let alone in our workplaces, our homes, our schools and our communities.

But there are influential organizations working to change this situation and publicize the new research. These include: the National Institute on Alcohol Abuse and Alcoholism (NIAAA), the National Institute on Drug Abuse (NIDA), the Substance Abuse and Mental Health Services Administration (SAMHSA), the World Health Organization (WHO), the American Medical Association (AMA) and the American Society of Addiction Medicine (ASAM).

And here is the especially good news when it comes to addiction treatment – the brain can and does change. See the image comparisons below.

SPECT Surface Scans of Brain During Substance Abuse (on Left) and One Year After Substance Abuse Stopped (on Right)

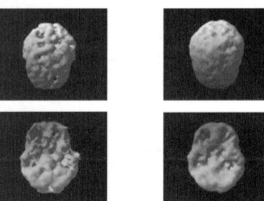

Image 3.2 SPECT Surface Scans During Substance Abuse and One Year After Substance Abuse Stopped. SPECT Surface Scans Courtesy of Amen Clinics, Inc.

Perhaps most importantly, this new research proves that addicts and alcoholics do not have to "hit bottom;" nor do they have to believe they have the disease of addiction; nor do they need to enter a treatment program voluntarily before they can begin treatment and successfully recover from their addictions.[8] This is a huge development in the field of addiction treatment. This means that courts, bosses, children, spouses, partners or significant others can do some "arm twisting" to get the alcoholic/addict into treatment – they do not have to wait until everything (and everyone) is falling apart. In fact, the earlier it happens, the better it is for treatment and recovery.[9] Of course, "arm twisting" *effectively* can make a world of difference. How to do this is something you will understand by the time you finish reading this book.

The Brain *Can* and *Does* Change

The following is an excerpt from "Challenges and Opportunities in Drug Addiction Research," by Dr. Nora Volkow, Director of the National Institute on Drug Abuse (NIDA), Dana Foundation:[10]

Neuroscience is at a historic turning point. Today, a full decade after the "Decade of the Brain," a continuous stream of advances is shattering long-held notions about how the human brain works and what happens when it doesn't. These advances are also reshaping the landscapes of other fields, from psychology to economics, education and the law.

Until the Decade of the Brain, scientists believed that, once development was over, the adult brain underwent very few changes. This perception contributed to polarizing perspectives on whether genetics or environment determines a person's temperament and personality, aptitudes, and vulnerability to mental disorders. But during the past two decades, neuroscientists have steadily built the case that the human brain, even when fully mature, is far more plastic—changing and malleable—than we originally thought.(1) It turns out that the brain (at all ages) is highly responsive to environmental stimuli and that connections between neurons are dynamic and can rapidly change within minutes of stimulation.

… For example, scientists are using imaging technologies in neurofeedback programs that train people to voluntarily recalibrate their neural activity in specific areas of the brain, allowing them to gain unprecedented control over, for example, pain perception(5) or emotional processing.(6) During drug addiction treatment, this approach could greatly reduce the risk of relapse by enabling a patient to control the powerful cravings triggered by a host of cues (e.g., people, things, places) that have become tightly linked, in the brain of the user, to the drug experience….

Checking items off the list...

(Refer to Chapter 1 for the full "Checklist of Next Steps For Family Members and Friends of an Addict or Alcoholic in [or Seriously Considering] Treatment.")

✔ **Learn about the explosion in brain research during the past 10-15 years.**

Points to Remember:

- Advances in brain imaging technologies of the past 10-15 years now allow scientists to study the live human brain. Imaging technologies, such as SPECT, enable scientists to observe areas of the brain that work well or that are low in activity or high in activity.

- These kinds of brain images provide the visual evidence of a clinical diagnosis and help people see that "something" happens in the brain as a result of substance abuse and/or addiction.

- These imaging technologies, and the resulting research they have made possible, underpin the clear, scientifically-based definition of addiction (to drugs or alcohol) as "a chronic, often relapsing brain disease."

- Addicts/alcoholics do not have to "hit bottom," nor believe they have the disease of addiction, nor enter a treatment program voluntarily in order for treatment and recovery to be successful.

CHAPTER 4

Understanding Neural Networks Helps Explain Why Addiction Is a Brain Disease

Even though government agencies and leading scientists now define addiction as a brain disease, you may not fully accept this claim. Or, you might be wondering how drinking and/or using drugs can possibly cause the disease. Or does it? How long does it take? Can anybody develop an addiction?

To answer these questions, it helps to understand that a brain disease occurs when "something" changes the normal functioning of the brain.

"How can drugs and alcohol create the 'something' that can cause a brain disease?" you might ask. The key to this answer is to understand how the brain develops and how it works. And the key to *that* understanding is to learn a bit about neural networks.

Suggestion: You are going to be seeing a lot of technical information in the next few chapters, so try reading it as you would a novel – nothing to struggle with, just a worthwhile read to pick up and set down as time and interest allows.

Neural Networks Explained

Basically, neural networks are neurons "talking" to one another. Neurons are the information processing units of the body's nervous system.[11] There are three types of neurons: *sensory neurons*, which bring information into the brain; *interneurons*, which process information *within* the brain; and *motor neurons*, which carry information *out* of the brain to the body's muscles.[12]

Essentially neural networks are neurons talking to one another. Understanding neural networks helps us to unlock the secrets of addiction and its impacts on family members and friends.

Neurons in the brain are also called brain cells. Neural networks in the brain control everything we think, feel, say and do. This is what makes the brain's neural networks of particular interest in terms of understanding how addiction is characterized as a brain disease.

In very general terms, neurons "talk" to one another through cues, electrical signals, branchlike extensions, neurotransmitters, synapses and receptors as follows:

■ A **cue**, which can be something like a sound, memory, touch, sight or smell, triggers a neuron to send an electrical signal.

Neuron to Neuron - Creating a Neural Network

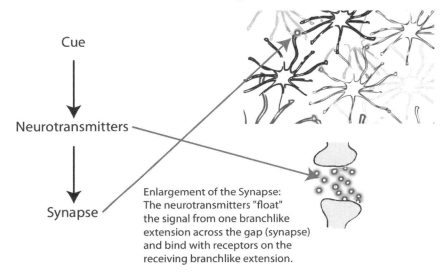

Image 4.1 Forming of a Neural Network. Courtesy Irene E. Yu

Please understand this is strictly a demonstrative illustration. An actual neural network is far more complicated and beyond the scope of this book.

■ The **electrical signal** travels down one of the neuron's **branchlike extensions,** where it triggers the release of the neurotransmitters stored there. The outgoing extensions are called *axons* and the incoming ones are called *dendrites*.

■ **Neurotransmitters** are chemical messengers that "float" the electrical signal across the gap between two branchlike extensions. The gap is called a **synapse**. The neurotransmitters bind with **receptors** on the receiving neuron's branchlike extension – something like a key fitting into a door lock.[13] The "message" is then converted back to an electrical signal and travels up the dendrite to the receiving neuron. That neuron may send its own electrical signal and continue the process or end the message.

Without neurotransmitters and receptors, one neuron cannot "talk" to another.

Putting it all together, the *cue* triggers an *electric signal* in the *axon* that then stimulates the release of "packets" of information (a.k.a. the signal message) that are floated across the *synapse* by the *neurotransmitters* to bind to *receptors* on the *dendrites* of the receiving neuron.

LOVED ONE IN TREATMENT? NOW WHAT!

This "talking" is known as a neural network. There can be hundreds of synapses on any one neuron, and there can be hundreds of thousands of synapses occurring in the brain at any one time.

Why It Is So Important to Understand Neural Networks

Neural networks are important to understand because everything we do – including addictions and reactions to secondhand drinking/drugging – is governed by how our neurons (brain cells) make those "talking" connections. Similarly, "our thoughts and behavior and environment reflect back on our neurons [brain cells]," which in turn influences "the pattern of connections."[14] In other words, it's the connections that make us who we are. Yet, and this point is crucial, we can also create and/or change those connections!

Some neural networks are instinctual, such as breathing, eating when hungry, drinking water when thirsty or the fight-or-flight reaction. Some neural networks are formed by repetitive activation, such as learning to ride a bike or speaking a new language or typing on a computer.

"Neurons that fire together wire together." (Shatz) If repeatedly activated, neural networks become embedded as "brain maps" for specific activities that "run" on "automatic pilot" when triggered into action.

Neuroscientist Carla Shatz summarizes this as follows: "Neurons that fire together wire together."[15] This firing together causes us to form embedded "brain maps"[16] [neurons that fired together, wired together] for everything we do. Think of these brain maps as well-worn pathways triggered into action by a cue – a memory, sound, sight, smell, touch, word or song. Some examples of brain maps include those we might develop for running (stride, foot strike, arm pump, breathing rhythm) or giving a presentation (voice inflections, hand gestures, facial expressions).

Thank Goodness for Synapses

Synapses allow brain maps to operate "one" at a time, instead of all at once.

Just think. If there were no synapses (gaps), then all of our neural networks would be stuck in the "on" position. We would be trying to sleep, sit, talk, run, read, do math, eat... ALL at once. Thus, the health of what happens at these synapses is critical to the brain's "thinking" and thereby to the body's overall health and functioning. Too much or not enough of a neurotransmitter, not enough receptors, unhealthy neurons or too much or not enough of some of the other key components to a successful neural transmission (which are too complicated to discuss here) can negatively impact the health of our neural networks and therefore the overall health of our brains. The underlying causes for these variances can be genetics, a brain injury or an illness, but they can also be the result of substance abuse, mental illness, addiction, poor nutrition, lack of exercise – even lack of sleep!

This information gives us power; **the power to change our neural networks and thereby change our thoughts, behaviors and actions.** In other words, understanding how a neural network is formed and becomes part of an embedded brain map helps us better understand how an established network pattern can prevent *other* neural network changes from occurring.[17]

Now the questions are: "How do we change established network patterns? How do we re-wire a brain map?" For this, we turn to the discussion of how our neural networks become established in the first place.

But first, take a moment to look at image 4.2 in the next section. It will help you better understand which neural networks control which activities – important information as we move forward.

Different Areas of the Brain Control Different Areas of Human Activities

Science has organized the brain into three general regions or "sub-brains." The neural networks in each sub-brain are involved in a different, over-all scope of human activity as described below. These sub-brains follow the pattern of the brain's evolution and development.

> *The Cerebellum is the "motor control" part of the brain; the Limbic System is the "reactionary" part of the brain; and the Cerebral Cortex is the "thinking" part of the brain.*

Note: Within each sub-brain, there are many, many parts. In the Limbic System alone, for example, there is the *amygdala, hippocampus* and *hypothalamus*, to name a few. Additionally, the sub-brains are also referred to by various names. The Cerebellum, for example, is often called the Reptilian brain. The primary objective of Image 4.2 is to help you understand there are three general groupings of brain activity.

The "3-Brain" Brain Complex

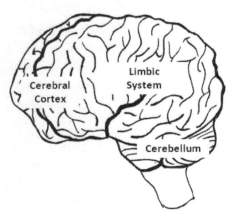

Cerebellum – the "motor control" part of our brains: *breathing, heartbeat and motor skills*

Limbic System – the "reactionary" part of our brains: *emotions, fight-or-flight, pleasure/reward and pain*

Cerebral Cortex – the "thinking" part of our brains: *reasoning, judgment, motivation, perception, memory and learning*

Image 4.2 The "3-Brain" Brain Complex / Key Brain Activities
Courtesy Jessica Scott

LOVED ONE IN TREATMENT? NOW WHAT!

You have just been given a crash course in neural networks and may be wondering why this matters – what can it possibly have to do with understanding addiction? The details will be explained in the next several chapters, but for now, review the "points to remember" listed below.

Checking items off the list...

✔ **Learn how the new brain research and study findings are revolutionizing our understanding of addiction (continued in Chapter 5).**

Points to Remember:

- Neurons are the information processing units of the body's nervous system. In the brain, neurons are also known as brain cells.

- Neurons "talking" to one another are called neural networks. Neurons, neurotransmitters, branchlike extensions (axons and dendrites), cues, electrical signals, synapses and receptors all work together to create a neural network.

- Neural networks in the brain control everything we think, feel, say and do.

- Brain maps are a series of neural networks that fire together. When repeatedly activated, they become embedded and flow without a great deal of thought when triggered by a cue. When we run, for example, we are following our brain map for running without really "thinking" too hard about what all has to happen in order for us to run.

- The health of the various components of a neural network are critical to the brain's "thinking" and thereby the body's overall health and functioning.

- Our thoughts, behaviors and environment greatly affect our neural networks and how they wire. By the same token, how our neural networks are wired greatly affects our thoughts and behaviors.

CHAPTER 5

The Wiring of Our Brains and
What It Means for Addiction

We are born with approximately 100 billion brain cells (neurons), but only a relatively small number are "wired" at birth.[18] This makes sense when you think about it. If our neural networks were all wired, we would come out walking and talking, doing math and being capable of reading literature or playing a musical instrument! Obviously that's not the case. About all we can do at birth is breathe, sleep, cry, suck, pee and poop.

Early Brain Development

From birth to about age three, our neurons wire at an explosive rate, guided primarily by our responses to touch, sound, sight, smell and taste. After all, we aren't reading at age two, so we cannot learn from a book or instruction on a computer. This means long before our conscious memories are formed, our brains are wiring in response to what is happening around and to us.

During the first three years of life, we "learn" by the way our neural networks wire in response to touch, sound, sight, smell and taste.

Then from about age four until puberty, our neural networks continue to wire and rewire. Think of this in terms of our newfound abilities to engage in sports, math, languages or playing music. In this first decade of life, a child's brain forms trillions of neural networks.[19]

And, then… just at the time when science used to think the work of brain development was "done" – "hardwired" – it turns out that the brain actually goes through another developmental process beginning around puberty and continuing through a person's early twenties (often through age 25!).[20] This new knowledge is only possible as a result of the advances made during the Decades of the Brain and Discovery.

Brain Development Ages 12 and Up

Image 5.1 below shows a 10-year, time-lapse study of brain development from ages 5 to 20 conducted by Dr. Paul Thompson and his NIMH/UCLA Project team at the University of California Los Angeles Laboratory of Neuro Imaging.

Above the line are side-view images and below the line are top-down images. The darker areas represent brain maturity. You may wish to visit <http://www.loni. ucla.edu/~thompson/DEVEL/PR.html> to view this in color.

There are three key developmental actions occurring in the brain during this time period:

1) Puberty. Puberty triggers a host of new hormonal and physical changes and neural networks.

2) Continued development of the cerebral cortex – the "thinking" part of our brain. This involves neural networks wiring within the Cerebral Cortex – the idea of learning calculus vs. memorizing multiplication tables, for example. It also involves neural networks in the Cerebral Cortex wiring to those in other areas of the brain – the idea of controlling emotions, which originate in the Limbic System, with logical thought, which originates in the Cerebral Cortex, for example.

Alcohol impacts a young person's brain differently than it does an adult brain. This is because of three brain developmental milestones occurring from ages 12 through 20, often through age 25!

3) "Pruning" and "strengthening" of neural networks.

Scientists now understand that all of this brain activity profoundly influences a young person's vulnerability to substance abuse and/or addiction.

Scans of Brain Development, Ages 5 – 20

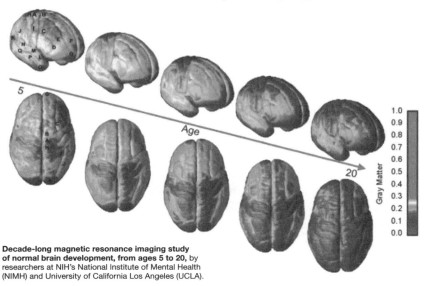

Decade-long magnetic resonance imaging study of normal brain development, from ages 5 to 20, by researchers at NIH's National Institute of Mental Health (NIMH) and University of California Los Angeles (UCLA).

Image 5.1 Brain Development, Ages 5 – 20
Courtesy Paul M. Thompson, Ph.D., Laboratory of Neuro Imaging, UCLA, NIMH/UCLA Project.

LOVED ONE IN TREATMENT? NOW WHAT!

The "pruning" and "strengthening" process is fascinating. Recall how the wiring of neural networks takes place during the first decade of life (as explained in the discussion earlier in this chapter). Everything a child experienced caused at least a "rough draft" of a neural network or else it would not have been possible. With the new neural networks brought on by puberty and cerebral cortex development described above (coupled with the stress that goes along with being an adolescent experiencing many transitional milestones [driving, high school, college, first job]), it is as if the brain "knows" it's on overload. So it starts a pruning and strengthening process commonly known as the "use it or lose it"[21] stage of brain development.

Neurons (grey matter) that are not being used are "pruned," and branchlike extensions (cabling or white matter) that *are* being used are "strengthened." This strengthening process involves "coating"' the branchlike extensions in myelin to make the neural connections more efficient. This allows messages to travel at 10 times the speed of non-myelinated extensions[22] – similar to the idea of an insulated cable wire being a better conductor than a non-insulated one.

During the "use it or lose it" stage of brain development that takes place in adolescence and young adulthood, the neural networks that are being used are strengthened. Those not being used are pruned.

If a young person repeatedly abuses alcohol or drugs during this developmental stage, the neural networks associated with memories and experiences related to substance misuse will be the ones <u>strengthened and embedded</u>. At the same time, neural networks damaged or not used because of the substance misuse will be <u>pruned</u>.

In other words, if young people spend their time seeking, consuming, abusing, hiding and recovering from substance misuse, then the neural networks used for those activities will be strengthened. And the neural networks not being used for other activities because of the focus on drugs or alcohol misuse – activities such as learning, sports or problem solving, for example – will be pruned. It's not that they "die" necessarily; rather, the brain misses some important neural network developing and strengthening opportunities.

Additionally, because the brain is NOT fully developed in young people, adolescents are more vulnerable than adults to many of the effects of alcohol, such as memory and learning.[23] This vulnerability of the young brain is something else we did not know until this new brain research. It also helps explain why teens don't know why it is they do some

Brain maps related to substance misuse are more easily embedded as a result of the brain development that occurs from ages 12 through 20, often through age 25.

of the things they do and why they take risks they likely would not engage in if they had a fully developed brain and the hindsight (memories and experiences) to go with it.

Early Use – One of the Key Risk Factors for Developing the Disease of Addiction

What science now understands is that addiction is a developmental disease –meaning it doesn't just strike one day – and it typically begins in childhood or adolescence.[24]

Early use is such a problem because of the brain development that is occurring (just described in the section above). Because the cerebral cortex is the last part of the brain to more fully develop, the neural networks therein – like those needed to assess situations, make sound decisions and keep our emotions and desires under control – are especially vulnerable to the effects of alcohol and/or drugs.

Additionally, the fact that this critical part of an adolescent's brain is still "a work-in-progress" puts them at increased risk for poor decisions (such as drinking or using drugs). Therefore, abusing drugs/alcohol while the brain is still developing may have profound and long-lasting consequences.[25]

> *Early use, independent of other risk factors, strongly predicts the development of alcoholism. (NIAAA)*

Unfortunately, society condones and often supports underage drinking as "something all kids go through" or accepts excuses such as, "remember when we were their age…," or "I'd rather they drink at my house so I know they're safe." This makes it easier to "mask" the problem and virtually promote the drinking/drugging that can cause the kinds of chemical and structural changes shown in Image 3.1.

Here are some facts about early use and alcoholism and why the risks and repercussions of underage drinking must be taken seriously:

- Early use, independent of other risk factors, strongly predicts the development of alcohol dependence, a.k.a. alcoholism. Of all people who have met the diagnostic criteria for alcoholism in their lifetime, nearly half were addicted by age 21 and two-thirds by age 25.[26] (NIAAA, "Snapshot of Underage Drinking")

- Young adults ages 18-20 have the highest rate of alcohol dependence (alcoholism) in the United States.[27] (U.S. Surgeon General 2007 Call to Action to Prevent and Reduce Underage Drinking)

And, by the way, contrary to common belief, the Europeans do not have the issue of underage drinking figured out, either. It is a significant problem in many European countries. You can read more about this in the *U.S. Surgeon General's Call to Action* referenced in this side-bar and cited in the Endnotes at the back of this book.

Far From Hardwired and What This Means for Addiction Treatment

This new brain research, then, has debunked another long-held belief – the one that declared our brains were hardwired by around puberty and that from that point on, it was in a long, slow process of decline. Not only that, but this research also shows the brain can form new nerve cells via neurogenesis.[28] And what all of this means for addiction treatment is profound!

Addicts and alcoholics can use this new science to actually change their brains – a concept known as **"neuroplasticity."** As Dr. Norman Doidge writes in his book, *The Brain That Changes Itself,* "Ironically, some of our most stubborn habits and disorders are products of our [brain's] plasticity. Once a particular plastic change occurs in the brain and becomes well established, it can prevent other changes from occurring. It is by understanding both the positive and negative effects of [the brain's] plasticity that we can truly understand the extent of human possibilities."[29]

In other words, by rewiring our neural networks, people can change their brains and thereby change their behaviors. And, this is what treatment is all about – helping addicts/alcoholics rewire their brains (discussed further in Chapter 8).

> *Effective addiction treatment must provide the tools that can help an addict/alcoholic rewire their brains.*

Equally important, family members and friends can now understand that their loved one's drinking/drugging behaviors were the result of chemical and structural changes in their brains. These *substance misuse behaviors were not a choice;* it was not *them.* But first, there is another piece to the puzzle to better explain this last statement and answer the question, "Why do some people become alcoholics/addicts and others do not?" In other words, "What 'causes' addiction?"

Checking items off the list...

✔ **Learn how the new brain research and study findings are revolutionizing our understanding of addiction (continued from Chapter 4).**

Points to Remember:

- Only a relatively small fraction of our brain cells are wired at birth. Trillions of neural networks are established during the first decade of life, which means early childhood experiences can have a profound effect on early brain development.

- Early use of drugs or alcohol is especially problematic because of the critical brain developmental processes that occur between ages 12 and 20, often continuing through age 25. It is one of the key risk factors for developing the disease of addiction.

- The brain is not "hardwired." A person can change their brains by improving the health of their neural networks (stopping substance abuse, for example) or changing their thoughts and behaviors. By the same token, rewiring one's brain will change a person's behaviors.

CHAPTER 6

How Substances of Abuse Hijack the Brain

All drugs of addiction – alcohol, heroin, marijuana, to name a few – target the pleasure/reward neural networks in the Limbic System.[30] Pleasure/reward neural networks allow us to enjoy eating a good meal, watching a football game or going on a date. They are what give us the feelings of contentment or happiness that make us want to repeat a behavior to get those feelings again. These neural networks are also responsible for many of our instinctual, hardwired survival activities, such as the drive to eat food when hungry or to drink water when thirsty.

How Drugs and Alcohol Hijack the Brain

The pleasure/reward neural networks rely on the neurotransmitter, dopamine. As you would guess, then, abusing drugs and alcohol interferes with what goes on at the dopamine synapses. Once a person starts to interrupt the health of their neural networks, the ripple effects are astounding.

Think of it as what happens during a traffic accident. All it takes is for two cars to slam into each other and traffic gets backed-up. Everything slows to a crawl in both directions, quickly changing normal traffic patterns on feeder streets or shutting down lanes entirely. And if the cars collided with a power line, entire neighborhoods are without electricity and on it goes. It's a mess! This same kind of ripple effect happens when substance misuse "slams into" the dopamine synapses of the pleasure/reward neural networks.

No dopamine, no pleasure. Dopamine is the neurotransmitter that makes pleasure/reward neural networks possible. Those networks are what allow us to experience feelings of contentment and happiness, which in turn makes us want to repeat the behavior in order to get the good feelings, again.

In moderation, drugs of addiction leave a person with a pleasurable feeling as the reward for the substance use. That feeling is what makes a person want to drink or use again. Let's face it – if drinking alcohol or using a drug did not make us feel good, it's unlikely we would repeat the behavior. In excess, the substance goes directly to the dopamine and "kicks it and kicks it and kicks it."[31] This "kicking" of the dopamine causes surges of dopamine in the synapses.

The brain – being the wonder that it is – dials down the dopamine, just like turning down the volume on a radio dial, and/or it reduces the number of receptors that can receive the dopamine-related signals.[32] This causes major interruptions at the synapses.

These neural network interruptions then ripple along to other neural networks thereby impacting other brain activities. Not only that, but the neural networks responsible for other activities are also suffering their own difficulties due to the alcohol or drug's independent impact on those synapses. All of this partially explains why repeated substance abuse results in the chemical and structural changes that in turn affect a person's thoughts and behaviors. In the case of alcohol abuse, the structural changes can be viewed in Image 3.1.

> *Alcohol or drug abuse interrupts the normal functioning of neural networks and eventually causes chemical and structural changes in the brain. These changes in turn alter the way the brain works, especially with regards to pleasure, judgment, decision making, learning and memory. (NIDA)*

Collectively, these chemical and structural changes alter the way the brain works, especially with regards to pleasure, judgment, decision making, learning and memory.[33] For addicts/alcoholics, these kinds of interruptions of the dopamine neural networks can make it very difficult to feel any pleasure from things they previously enjoyed.[34]

The Illusion of Control – the Disease of Addiction

Meanwhile, if a person crosses the invisible line from abuse to addiction (for reasons to be explained shortly), there is "an adaptation, that tells the brain this drug [or alcohol] is indispensable for survival."[35] Not understanding this fact, the addict/alcoholic drinks/uses even more trying to get the "feel good feeling."

But that feeling is no longer possible because the brain has dialed down the dopamine and/or reduced receptors. So where do alcoholics/addicts turn to feel joy at a wedding or sadness at a funeral? Alcohol or drugs. What makes spending time with the family special? Alcohol or drugs. What is the thing that makes them want to get out of bed, and what makes them feel good after a bad day at the office? Alcohol or drugs. But in time, even the alcohol or drugs don't do the trick because of the vicious spiral of addiction, which is described next.

> *Addicts/alcoholics experience cravings for their drugs or alcohol that are five times more powerful than their instinctual cravings for food or water. (Riggs)*

The disease of addiction, as opposed to the condition of substance abuse, is characterized by substance misuse behaviors AND the following four symptoms:

Cravings – the strong, overpowering need and urge to drink or use. Addiction cravings are "five times stronger than the [instinctual] cravings our brains evolved in the first place to be rewarded by, like food or water or sex."[36] These cravings explain why an alcoholic/addict will lie, steal, cheat, sneak, intimidate a loved one – do anything to get and use their substance. It can perhaps help you understand that your loved one meant it when he or she tearfully told you with heartfelt sincerity for the umpteenth time, "I'm so, so sorry. I love you so much. I promise I'll stop. I promise." Now you can better understand it was: 1) the compromised dopamine neural networks that "told" them their substance was "indispensable for survival," *and* 2) the changes in other areas of the brain critical for judgment, decision making, learning, memory and behavior control that, combined with #1, overrode your loved one's self control.[37] It was not *them*.

Loss of Control – the inability to predictably control and/or stop once substance use has begun. Loss of control is further defined by the persistent desire but unsuccessful efforts to cut down and the crazed obsession with trying to obtain, use, hide and/or recover from the effects of their substance of choice. Not understanding their neural networks have been hijacked by drugs or alcohol tricks addicts/alcoholics (and often their family and friends) into believing they can control how much they use. Recognizing and accepting this loss of control is what it means to be "powerless over alcohol (or drugs)."

Physical Dependence – the body physically comes to depend on the drug or alcohol. Recall the explanation in Chapter 2 of how alcohol "sits" in the body's tissues with high water content while it waits to be metabolized by the liver, for example. If an alcoholic/addict stops drinking/using, s/he may experience withdrawal symptoms, such as nausea, sweating, shakiness and anxiety. They may try using another substance to relieve or avoid the withdrawal symptoms. Physical dependence is why some addicts/alcoholics need to go through a medically supervised detoxification/stabilization process (a.k.a. detox).

Both substance abuse and addiction cause chemical and structural changes in the brain. Both result in substance misuse behaviors, which in turn cause secondhand drinking/drugging impacts. However, addiction differs from substance abuse because of the four symptoms that characterize the disease: cravings, loss of control, physical dependence and tolerance.

Tolerance – having to consume greater amounts of the substance to get the same "buzz." (Remember the seeking of that buzz is triggered by embedded neural networks, but the brain is unable to experience the "feel good feelings" because dopamine has been dialed down and/or dopamine receptors have been reduced.) The addict/alcoholic drinks/uses more in an attempt to capture the "feel good feeling" – the "dopamine high" – but it is a high that is no longer possible.[38]

Among the four symptoms that characterize the disease of addiction described above, notice the word, "predictably," used in the section on "Loss of Control." Yes, addicts/alcoholics may be able to stop for days, weeks, even years or to use intermittently. And at times, they may seem to hold it to a reasonable amount. All of which gives everyone concerned the illusion that the addict/alcoholic has their drinking/drugging under their control.

This illusion helps explain why you believed your loved one when he or she promised to stop or cut down because it appeared as if s/he could! But all it may take is one drink, one hit, one snort or one pill to activate the embedded addiction-related neural networks in any given area of the brain (memory, judgment and perception in the Cerebral Cortex, pleasure/reward in the Limbic System, for example). And, given the cravings, physical dependence, tolerance and loss of control characteristics of addiction, the addict/alcoholic cannot predictably control the outcome of that one drink, one hit, one snort or one pill.

This is why addicts/alcoholics must abstain completely if they want to be able to change their brains and therefore stop their substance misuse behaviors long-term. It is also why addiction can be a relapsing disease because if an addict/alcoholic uses again, thinking they can control it this time or these many years later, they will find themselves caught in the spiral of the addiction once more. Therefore, abstaining is the only option that will allow them to control/stop their substance misuse behaviors long-term. It is also the only thing that will allow their dopamine neurotransmitter levels and receptors to come back. As you will learn in Chapter 8, treatment and recovery can help an addict/alcoholic successfully abstain.

An alcoholic/addict is incapable of predictably controlling their intake, and therefore their substance misuse behaviors, as long as they drink/use ANY amount.

The Effects of Commonly Abused Substances on the Brain

Source: NIDA, "How Drugs Affect the Brain," National Institute on Drug Abuse (NIDA) of the National Institutes of Health (NIH), last updated 9/19/08, <http://www.drugabuse.gov/JSP/MOD6/page3.html>

Cocaine. When someone snorts, injects, or smokes cocaine, it travels to the brain very quickly. It reaches all areas of the brain but has its greatest effects in the front part of the cerebral cortex and on part of the limbic system.

A very complicated process takes place in the brain after it is exposed to cocaine. In a normal brain, the neurotransmitter dopamine is released by neurons to carry messages in the limbic system. After the message has been carried to the next neuron, dopamine is reabsorbed from the synapse back into the neuron that released it. Cocaine blocks the reabsorption of dopamine, leaving too much dopamine in the synapse. The excess dopamine is what causes the pleasurable feelings associated with taking cocaine and the increased motor activity seen with higher doses.

After a person abuses cocaine for a while, the brain tries to compensate for the excess dopamine, and the normal processes that take place are disrupted. The brain will no longer function normally without cocaine.

Marijuana. The active ingredient in marijuana that produces changes in brain messages is called tetrahydrocannabinol (THC). The brain has receptors for a specific chemical, anandamide, which is naturally produced by the brain. THC is able to attach to and activate these same receptors. When a person uses marijuana, the chemicals in the drug travel through the bloodstream and attach to the THC receptors, activating them and interfering with normal neurotransmission.

The areas of the brain with the most THC receptors are the cerebellum, the cerebral cortex, and the limbic system. This is why marijuana affects thinking, problem solving, sensory perception, movement, balance, and memory.

Alcohol. The parts of the brain affected by alcohol are the cerebral cortex, limbic system, and brain stem [Cerebellum]. Alcohol interferes with messages carried by many neurotransmitters in the brain. Because these neurotransmitters are found throughout the brain, alcohol affects many functions, including thinking, coordination, and emotions.

Side-Effects of Various Drugs

Source: Medline Plus, "Drug Dependence," U.S. National Library of Medicine and the National Institute of Medicine, National Institutes of Health, <http://www.nlm.nih.gov/medlineplus/ency/article/001522.htm>

Opiates and narcotics are powerful painkillers that cause drowsiness (sedation) and feelings of euphoria. These include heroin, opium, codeine, meperidine (Demerol), hydromorphone (Dilaudid) and oxycodone (Oxycontin).

Central nervous system stimulants include amphetamines, cocaine, dextroamphetamine, methamphetamine and methylphenidate (Ritalin). These drugs have a stimulating effect, and people can start needing higher amounts of these drugs to feel the same effect (tolerance).

Central nervous system depressants include alcohol, barbiturates (amobarbital, pentobarbital, secobarbital), benzodiazepine (Valium, Ativan, Xanax), chloral hydrate, and paraldehyde. These substances produce a sedative and anxiety-reducing effect, which can lead to dependence.

Hallucinogens include LSD, mescaline, psilocybin ("mushrooms") and phencyclidine (PCP or "angel dust"). They can cause people to see things that aren't there (hallucinations) and can lead to psychological dependence.

Tetrahydrocannabinol (THC) is the active ingredient found in marijuana (cannabis) and hashish. Although used for their relaxing properties, THC-derived drugs can also lead to paranoia and anxiety.

Denial. A Key Reason for the Progression of Substance Abuse and/or the Disease of Addiction

One of the keys to the progression of a loved one's drinking or drug use going from bad to worse, sliding from abuse to addiction, is DENIAL. Denial is a very human defense mechanism we all use at one time or another to protect ourselves from facing something we just don't want to face. It can be seen in the expression of a guilty four-year old who denies breaking a vase for fear of being punished, or in the eyes of a lover who doesn't want to admit the relationship is over or in the dieter's pretending the size of a piece of birthday cake doesn't really matter.

For alcoholics/addicts, however, denial not only distorts reality and hurts other people, it can ultimately result in death. For substance abusers, denial can lead to addiction and/or years of destructive substance misuse behaviors. Denial is what causes the substance abuser/alcoholic/addict to adopt an arsenal of offensive measures (anger, minimizing, rationalizing, blaming and deceiving) in order to protect his or her ability to drink or use.

> *An addict/alcoholic's denial can range from flimsy excuses to devious lies, whether the addict/alcoholic claims they "accidentally" hid a bottle in a gym bag, or their friend had an "emergency" and needed their help or they were "just holding the pot and paraphernalia for a friend."*

And, for family members, denial is what causes them to adopt unhealthy coping skills (such as striving to be all things to all people so that the loved one won't drink/use; working hard to get good grades and stay out of trouble so mom/dad won't have one more thing to deal with, etc.). These coping skills allow the family member or friend to excuse or rationalize or defend themselves against the substance misuse behaviors, telling themselves things like, "Everyone drinks too much now and again." "Lots of people drink and drive – he just got caught." "Pot is not that bad, at least he's not using heroin." Family members or friends in denial can aide (without even understanding they are) in the progression of a loved one's substance misuse. But more importantly, they can wreak havoc in their own lives – not only emotionally but often physically as well, experiencing conditions such as anxiety, depression, inadequate sleep and so on.

Together, the person drinking/using drugs and those who love him or her collaborate to enforce and support the notion that what is going on is not really what is going on. They do this to avoid labeling loved ones as people with a drinking or drug problem they cannot control – or worse yet, of being alcoholics/addicts.

And so, together they continue to enforce the two most important rules in a household where substance misuse occurs and/or where a loved one has crossed the line to addiction:

Rule #1: Alcohol/drug use is not the problem.

Rule #2: Do not talk to anyone (not family, not friends) about the drinking/ drug use nor the behaviors related to the substance misuse. Above all, attack, minimize or discredit any family member or friend who does.

Denial becomes automatic because the thought processes develop into embedded neural networks. One way to recognize denial is to listen for the words, "*but...*" and "*yeah but...,*" as in, "He drank, *but* he was never mean to me." "*Yeah*, he smoked pot, *but* then how is that different from someone having a few drinks?" "She broke her promise to stop drinking if I paid her rent, *but* if I don't pay her rent, she'll be homeless." "I wouldn't have had so much to drink, *but* the kids' fighting was getting on my nerves!"

Listen for the words, "but," and "yeah but." These are generally a sign your thought process is stuck in denial.

Unless and until alcoholics/ addicts, family members and friends break through their denial, the consequences of a loved one's drinking or drug use will continue to spiral, and together, they will "all fall down." It only gets worse. It cannot/will not get better until the denial ends. Family members and friends will better understand the concept of denial by reading Chapters 10-12, where they will also find suggestions for what to do about it.

One wife said, "It wasn't until he tried to strangle me in front of the kids that I left him. Yet the verbal abuse I took from him and the insane arguments we'd get into when he was drunk left me a wreck for days. But I would always try to make it okay in my mind, like 'this time it'll be different.' For some reason, being physically attacked made it 'okay' to finally leave. Oh! And get a load of this – he said he'd be willing to take me back if I'd apologize for making him mad enough to attack me. And to think I used to try to make sense of that kind of logic!"

Assess Your Loved One's Addiction Characteristics/ Substance Misuse Behaviors

Give some thought to the following questions[39] and try to answer them as fully as possible. You do not have to write the answers here, but you certainly may if you'd like. Completing this informal assessment may help you break through your denial and better understand your loved one's behaviors are the consequences of their disease.

- How long has your loved one's substance misuse been a problem for you? ___ 1-3 years ___ 4 – 6 years ___ 7 – 10 years ___ longer ___ I don't know, I didn't really think there was a problem

- Approximately how much does your loved one drink / use on a typical occasion?

- What's the greatest amount consumed on an occasion that you are aware of?

Note: Family members and friends are often not aware of the alcohol or drug use, especially when it comes to drug use. When presented with the fact that their loved one is in or is contemplating treatment, they are especially confused. "How could this be?" they ask. And when they learn the extent and duration of use, they are shocked. Then they are often plagued by thoughts like, "How could I not know?"

For those family members and friends who were not aware of the drug or alcohol abuse, the remainder of this assessment may or may not apply. It is likely, however, you did notice your loved one's behavioral changes – such as their being cranky, high strung, only sleeping 4-5 hours/night, always having a plausible reason for an implausible happening (for example, "I got the car because of some work I did for a guy."), changing friendships or losing interest in things they used to enjoy. If this is the case for you, try to go back and think about those kinds of "nagging-feeling" moments and write them down.

- Did you notice an increase in the amount they drank / used? Did it increase even more over time? ____N ____ Y ____ Wasn't aware

- Did you see times when s/he appeared to be drinking/using less than usual, yet s/he still seemed drunk or out of it? ____N ____ Y ____ sometimes

- Has your loved one let go of friendships and/or activities that don't include or support having alcohol/drug use? ____ N ____ Y ____ sometimes

- Does your loved one make excuses for not doing things s/he used to do, such as having friends over for dinner or going to a movie or doing sports in school? ____ N ____ sometimes ____ a lot

- Has your loved one ever taken money from you or lied about getting paid or spent money on their substance that you'd planned to spend on something else? ____ N ____ sometimes ____ often

- Does your loved one seem to change personalities or do things s/he normally wouldn't do when s/he misuses drugs/alcohol? ____ N ____Y. If yes, please check all that apply:
    - ____ gets loud, sometimes angry, shouting
    - ____ doesn't listen to what I say and tries to make it seem as if I'm the one who doesn't understand what we're talking about
    - ____ says mean, hurtful things
    - ____ makes me (or the children/siblings) afraid
    - ____ drives or drives with others in the car while under the influence
    - ____ tries to physically intimidate me (or the children/siblings)

____ sometimes hits me (or the children/siblings)

____ passes out

____ doesn't remember the next day what s/he did the night before

____ tries to pick a fight even when I try to stay out of his/her way or go into another room

____ insists on being intimate or having sexual relations when under the influence, even if I do not want to

____ does not come home or leaves the house after the substance misuse has started

____ other

- Has your loved one repeatedly tried and/or talked about wanting to stop his/her substance misuse? ____ N ____ Y

  If yes, did it work? ____ N ____ Y

  If yes, for how long? ____ Y ____ N What reason did he/she give (if any) for going back to using?

- Did your loved one lie to you, tell fantastical stories or give plausible excuses and/or reasons for bizarre behaviors (such as you finding a bottle of vodka tucked in their trunk, or their having lost track of time after stopping for a "couple of pops" with their friends or their claim the cocaine packet belonged to a friend who was trying to quit so wanted your loved one to hold it for him/her?) ____ N ____ Y ____ Sometimes ____ Often

- Did you notice your loved one would be shaky or anxious or complain of having eaten something that didn't sit well if s/he tried not to drink or use? ____ N ____ Y ____ Sometimes ____ Often

Checking items off the list...

✔ **Learn about the disease of addiction, whether it be an addiction to drugs or alcohol.**

Points to Remember:

- All drugs of addiction target the pleasure/reward neural networks in the Limbic System. These networks rely on the neurotransmitter, dopamine.

- Repeated substance abuse causes surges of dopamine, which in turn causes the brain to dial down the dopamine and/or reduce the number of dopamine receptors. In time, these changes can make it difficult for the addict/alcoholic to feel pleasure from normal activities they had previously enjoyed.

- Repeated substance abuse results in chemical and structural changes in the brain, which alter the way the brain works, especially with regards to pleasure, judgment, decision making, learning and memory.

- Addiction is different from substance abuse because of the four key characteristics of the disease of addiction: cravings, loss of control, physical dependence and tolerance. However, both substance abuse and addiction cause secondhand drinking/drugging impacts and substance misuse behaviors.

- Addicts/alcoholics are "powerless" over their ability to predictably control their substance use because of the characteristics of the disease of addiction; their brains have been hijacked.

- Denial is a key to the progression of the substance abuse and/or the disease of addiction. Because of denial, a person can move from substance *use* to *abuse* to *addiction*. Breaking through denial is a crucial step for treatment and recovery. Methods for breaking through denial are explained in Chapters 11 – 13.

- Completing an informal assessment of your loved one's addiction characteristics/substance misuse behaviors can help you break through your own denial and help you better understand that your loved one's addiction behaviors are the consequence of his/her brain disease.

CHAPTER 7

Why Do Some Substance Abusers Become Alcoholics/Addicts and Others Do Not?

It has been repeated time and again – substance abuse causes chemical and structural changes in the brain. But why do some people cross the invisible line from substance abuse to substance addiction? Why are some people able to drink or use abusively for the remainder of their lives and never cross that invisible line?

The new brain and substance abuse/addiction-related research makes it clear there are many factors that interact to produce different drinking or substance use patterns in people. The commonly recognized "causes of addiction" are a combination of biological, environmental and developmental risk factors. The more risk factors a person has, the more likely s/he is to develop the disease of addiction.

Common Risk Factors – "Causes" of Addiction

The most widely recognized common **risk factors**, described below, include genetics, social environment, mental illness, early use and childhood trauma.[40] Here's a closer look at each of these risk factors:

Social Environment. People who live, work or go to school in an environment where heavy drug or alcohol use is common – such as a family, workplace or school setting in which heavy drinking or using is seen as an important way to bond at family events, with co-workers or fellow students – are more likely to abuse substances, as well.

Mental Health Illness. Thirty-seven percent of alcohol abusers and fifty-three percent of drug abusers also have at least one serious mental illness,[41][42] such as depression, PTSD, bipolar, anxiety, schizophrenia. The common term for this condition in treatment circles is a "dual diagnosis," which refers to

Addiction is "caused by" a combination of biological, environmental and developmental risk factors. The key risk factors include: social environment, mental health illness, early use, genetics and childhood trauma. The more risk factors an individual has, the more likely that person's substance abuse will proceed to addiction.

someone having both a mental illness and an addiction. Often what happens is the person starts to drink or use drugs to self-medicate the mental illness. This

49

self-medication can sometimes make the mental illness worse; however it does not *cause* the mental illness. Mental illness is also a brain disease with its own brain changes. See Image 7.1.

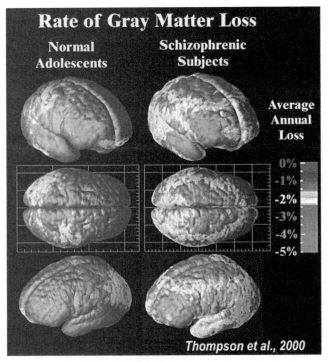

Image 7.1 Comparison of Normal Adolescent's Brain to Adolescent Schizophrenic Subject's Brain
Courtesy Dr. Paul Thompson, UCLA Laboratory of Neuro Imaging

Understanding the nature of mental illness and addiction makes it easier to understand that both the mental illness and the addiction must be treated at the same time (a process described in more detail in Chapter 8). Removing the substance – the "coping skill" – without replacing it with something else (such as treatment and/or medication for the mental illness), or treating the mental illness without treating the addiction, is a set-up for failure.

Early Use.   Because of the critical brain development that occurs from ages 12 through 20, often through 25, a young person's brain is especially vulnerable to the chemical and structural changes caused by substance misuse. Adults, ages 21 or older who started using alcohol before age 15, for example, were almost

Alcohol and drugs affect the developing brain DIFFERENTLY than they affect the brain of an adult.

six times more likely to have alcohol dependence or abuse than adults who first used alcohol at age 21 or older (15.1 percent vs. 2.6 percent).[43]

LOVED ONE IN TREATMENT? NOW WHAT!

<u>Genetics</u>. Just as with diabetes or heart disease, if a person has a family history of addiction, there is a greater likelihood s/he is genetically predisposed. Scientists estimate that genetic factors account for between 40 and 60 percent of a person's vulnerability to addiction.[44] Additionally, a person's genetic

Scientists estimate that genetic factors account for between 40 and 60 percent of a person's vulnerability to addiction. (NIDA)

make-up might include: lower or higher levels of a neurotransmitter(s); fewer receptors; a unique disease that affects neural networks; fewer of the liver enzymes that break down alcohol or any number of other genetic-based differences, such as gender and ethnicity.

<u>Childhood Trauma</u>. Abuse (such as verbal, physical or mental abuse) or child neglect; persistent conflict in the family (such as that surrounding a family member's unacknowledged alcohol abuse, drug addiction or mental illness); or sexual abuse and/or other traumatic childhood experiences can shape a child's brain chemistry (the way their neural networks wire) and subsequent vulnerability to substance misuse.[45]

Why Childhood Trauma and Social Environment are Such High Risk Factors

If you think about how the brain develops, it is easier to understand how growing up in a family where a loved one's substance abuse and/ or addiction is unacknowledged and/or untreated can cause a child's brain to wire unhealthy coping skills. These coping skills are triggered not only by the substance misuse behaviors but also by the secondhand drinking/ drugging behaviors of the other family members.

Families of individuals with alcohol use disorders are often characterized by conflict, chaos, communication problems, unpredictability, inconsistencies in messages to children, breakdown in ritual and traditional family rules, emotional and physical abuse.[46] (NIAAA, "Social Work Education for the Prevention and Treatment of Alcohol Use Disorders, Module 10J, Alcohol and the Family)

Further, a child growing up in a home with an addict/alcoholic sees that person's behavior and the non-drinking person's behavior as role models for what is acceptable. Additionally, the child will typically have easier access to the alcohol or drugs in their households. (And of course, genetics is also a risk factor for these children.) "Children's earliest interactions within the family are crucial to their healthy development and risk for drug abuse."[47]

Assessing Your Loved One's Risk Factors for the Disease of Addiction

Now that you've learned about the risk factors for developing the disease of addiction, it may help you to see how many of these risk factors apply to your loved one. To complete this informal assessment, give some thought to the following questions[48] and try to answer them as fully as possible. (You may need to use a separate piece of paper.)

Social Environment / Childhood Trauma / Genetics

• Has your loved one lost anyone close to him/her from death or abandonment or extended absences which were not understood by your loved one?
__Don't Know ___ N ___ Y

• Does anyone in his/her immediate family (parent, grandparent, sibling, child, spouse) suffer from an untreated or undiagnosed mental illness (depression, anxiety, bipolar, schizophrenia, post-traumatic stress disorder - PTSD)?
__ Don't Know __ N ____ Y

• Were there secrets (a parent's drinking or a mother's sadness or a sibling's drug use) – things which were not fully understood nor openly talked about – in your loved one's family that family members were expected to excuse, hide or not discuss? ___ Don't Know __ N ___Y

• Were there things that went on in your loved one's family of origin that did not seem right or normal (for example, a parent or sibling who raged or paid more or unusual attention to one child over another)? ___ Don't Know__ N ___ Y

• Did your loved one feel invisible in his/her family of origin (or in your present living arrangement), perhaps due to another family member's illness or disability that consumed the family's focus and attention? ___ Don't Know__ N ___ Y

• Were alcohol or drugs generally used at family functions or gatherings hosted by your loved one's parents for families and friends?
___ Don't Know ___ N ___ Y
If you know, did people drink to excess? ___ N ___ Y

Were young people allowed to drink? ___ Don't Know ___ N ___ Y

• Was a family member's drug or alcohol use a source of fighting or problems in your loved one's family of origin? ___ Don't know ___ N ___ Y

• Is there a history in your loved one's family of origin of:

　　Violence? ___ Don't know ___ N ___ Y

　　Arrests? ___ Don't know ___ N ___ Y

　　Verbal or Emotional Abuse? ___ Don't know ___ N ___ Y

　　Physical Abuse? ___ Don't know ___ N ___ Y

　　Sexual Abuse? ___ Don't know ___ N ___ Y

　　Other Trauma? ___ Don't know ___ N ___ Y

- Do you know if any members of your loved one's family of origin had an alcohol or illegal or prescription drug misuse problem? ___ Don't know ___ N ___ Y

  If yes, please check all that apply:

  ___ mother

  ___ father

  ___ grandparent, aunt, uncle, cousin

  ___ sibling

Mental Illness

- Has your loved one ever been diagnosed with a mental health illness or condition, such as ADHD, PTSD, anxiety, depression or bipolar?
  ___ Don't Know ___ N ___ Y

- Has your loved one ever talked with a psychiatrist, psychologist or counselor?
  ___ Don't Know ___ N ___ Y

  If yes, did he/she find it helpful?
  ___ Don't Know ___ N ___ Y

- Has your loved one ever felt s/he needed help for emotional problems or mental health issues (or have you or others suggested s/he seek help)?
  ___ Don't know ___ N ___ Y

- Has your loved one ever had nightmares or flashbacks or intensive thoughts as a result of some traumatic event? ___ Don't know ___ N ___ Y

- Has your loved one ever had times when he/she felt panicky, suddenly anxious, to the extent their heart beats rapidly or they begin to sweat and feel immobilized?
  ___ Don't know ___ N ___ Y

- Has your loved one ever been depressed for several weeks at a time or lost pleasure in work, school or other activities? ___ Don't Know ___ N ___ Y

- Did he/she ever attempt or threaten to kill him/herself?
  ___ Don't know ___ N ___ Y

- Has your loved one ever had periods of time when he/she had a high energy level, their ideas and thoughts came rapidly or when they needed little sleep?
  ___ Don't know ___ N ___ Y

- Has your loved one ever had periods of time when s/he seemed immobilized, spending significant periods of time in bed or hardly getting off the couch?
  ___ Don't know ___ N ___ Y

- Has your loved one ever had lasting thoughts or an impulse to do something over and over again that caused him/her distress or interfered with normal routines (checking something repeatedly, washing hands)? ___ Don't Know ___ N ___ Y

<u>Early Use</u>
- How old was your loved one when s/he first used drugs or alcohol? _____

- Did s/he continue to use after that first time? ___ Don't Know ___ N ___ Y

- How often did s/he use drugs or alcohol in middle school?
  _____ just once _____ couple of times _____ about once a quarter
  ___ monthly ___ weekly _____ daily

- How often did s/he use drugs or alcohol in high school?
  _____ just once _____ couple of times _____ about once a quarter
  ___ monthly ___ weekly _____ daily

- How often did s/he use drugs or alcohol in college or after graduation from high school?
  _____ just once _____ couple of times _____ about once a quarter
  ___ monthly ___ weekly _____ daily

- Did his/her parents offer, encourage and/or allow him/her to use alcohol or drugs at home before your loved one turned age 18?
  ___ Don't Know ___ N ___ Y

- Did his/her parents host parties at which alcohol or drugs were allowed in hopes of keeping his/her friends "safe"?
  ___ Don't Know ___ N ___ Y

- Did s/he engage in life-changing experiences as a result of his/her drug or alcohol use (for example, unwanted or unprotected sex, fights, arrests, DUI)?
  ___ Don't Know ___ N ___ Y

Checking items off the list...

✔ **Accept your loved one has the disease of addiction (if they do).**

Points to Remember:

- Addiction is "caused" by a combination of biological, developmental and environmental risk factors. The most common include: early use, mental illness, social environment, childhood trauma and genetics, and of course, substance abuse, which causes chemical and structural changes in the brain.

- Informally assessing your loved one's risk factors for developing the disease of addiction can help you further accept that s/he has it. (This kind of an informal assessment can also help you better appreciate why it will be important to talk to your children, so they might recognize their own risk factors and the effects of secondhand drinking/drugging they have experienced. Chapter 13 will help clarify these issues.)

CHAPTER 8

Treating Addiction for What it Is – A Chronic, Often Relapsing Brain Disease

You have probably been told something like, "Alcoholism / drug addiction is just like any other disease." After which you have probably said to yourself or to whomever made the statement, "Like *!?!#! it is! People with diabetes or heart disease don't steal money from me or endanger my children by driving while under the influence!"

And, you are correct in one sense. Other diseases, like diabetes and heart disease, for example, do not usually include the *kinds* of behavioral issues described in previous chapters. (There are behavioral factors, but not substance misuse behaviors.) Why? Because diseases like heart disease and diabetes are not brain diseases. They do not cause chemical and structural changes in the areas of the brain a person needs in order to think straight and act responsibly.

> *Addiction is a disease, which means it shares common characteristics with other diseases. But it is a brain disease, unlike many other diseases.*

So where is the common ground between addiction and other diseases, like diabetes and heart disease? Below you will find some of the common characteristics diseases share:

- They are <u>chronic</u>.

- They have the <u>potential to result in death</u> if untreated.

- There is a <u>genetic influence </u>associated with vulnerability.

- They involve <u>behavioral factors</u> associated with the onset of the disease.

- They have the <u>potential for relapse</u> if treatment recommendations are not followed.[49]

These similarities explain why effective addiction treatment requires a "disease management"[50] approach, as opposed to an acute care approach (i.e., "28-days and you're good to go"). While the components and deliveries will vary, because no single treatment component is appropriate for all individuals at all times,[51] the overall objectives of a disease management approach to addiction treatment should involve three phases: 1) detoxification/stabilization, 2) rehabilitation and 3) continuing care.[52]

Why Addiction Treatment Should Be Like Treating Other Chronic Diseases

The following highlights some of the concepts presented in the George Washington University Medical Center's paper, "Ensuring Solutions to Alcohol Problems, Primer 1, Executive Summary, Treating Alcoholism as a Chronic Disease."[53] While these are specific to the treatment of alcoholism, they also hold true for drug addictions.

• Treating patients with alcoholism, similar to treating patients with other chronic diseases, calls for them to follow treatment recommendations that include education, counseling, behavioral changes and medication.

• Treating chronic diseases is difficult, however, if patients do not follow through with implementing the recommended behavioral changes, in addition to taking any medications that have been prescribed. For example, 40% of patients with diabetes or high blood pressure and nearly 60% of those with diabetes take their medications, but less than a third of them are "able to make the behavioral changes necessary to improve their health and prevent re-occurrence of symptoms."

• When an alcoholic experiences a relapse, they are considered weak-willed, not committed, and treatment is viewed as having failed. This is not the case when treating patients with asthma, diabetes or high blood pressure who experience re-occurring symptoms. They are viewed as needing further or modified treatment.

• Treatment of diabetes, high blood pressure or asthma is viewed as ongoing, with continued monitoring and modifications. It is also out in the open. The same is not true with alcoholism, a disease generally treated in secrecy and shrouded in shame, with little ongoing medical follow-up. This is borne out in the way health insurance policies discriminate against alcoholism treatments vs. other chronic disease treatments. For example: "Medicare only pays 50 percent of outpatient treatment costs for alcoholism, compared to 80 percent for other diseases."

Three Phases of Successful Addiction Treatment

As you can imagine after reading thus far, treating a brain disease should focus on healing, changing and developing new neural networks in the brain, as well as restoring the body to physical health. With a disease management approach – one that involves detoxification/stabilization, rehabilitation and continuing care – recovery (defined as abstinence and a joy-filled life) is entirely within your loved one's control.

The three components or phases of a disease management approach to addiction treatment are briefly described below. The more detailed explanations of what is involved in each phase follows.

It is important to understand there is no "one size fits all" way to "do" addiction treatment. This can be frustrating for family members and friends (and the addicts/alcoholics), all of whom want a straightforward answer, like: "Follow A, B, C, then D, and you will get well." But, like treating other diseases, addiction treatment can be a bit of this and some of that and some trial and error. Nonetheless addiction treatment absolutely can work, and your loved one can go on to enjoy a wonderful

Addiction treatment requires a "disease management" approach. This includes three phases:
- detoxification/stabilization
- rehabilitation
- continuing care.
There are many options within each phase that a person can use. No "one size fits all" when it comes to addiction treatment.

life (and so can you!). Now for a brief overview of the three phases of the disease management approach to addiction treatment:

Detoxification / stabilization is the phase of treatment when alcohol and drugs are safely removed from the addict/alcoholic's system in order to physiologically stabilize him/her.

Rehabilitation (a.k.a. Rehab) is the phase of treatment where individuals start the process of changing their brains – repairing, developing new and rewiring old neural networks – while at the same time, restoring their body's physical health.

Generally rehab starts with an intense, almost immersion-like period, during which time the addict/alcoholic focuses on abstinence, education and behavioral changes. As neural networks change/repair/develop and physical health returns, rehabilitation efforts are generally changed and/or modified.

Continuing Care is the phase of treatment that follows rehabilitation. This is a plan, a specific strategy, for how the addict/alcoholic is going to continue and maintain abstinence *and* a joy-filled life after the detox/stabilization and rehabilitation phases have been completed.

A More Detailed Explanation of Phase 1: Detoxification/Stabilization

Detox may last anywhere from three to five days and up to five to seven weeks. It is safest if it is conducted under the guidance of a healthcare professional. To aid in this process, medicines may be prescribed or the substance may gradually be withdrawn (as

"This is how insane it was for me," said one alcoholic. "I wanted to get sober so that I could prove I could control my drinking!"

opposed to stopped abruptly). Or a medical substitute for the substance may be used, such as methadone being prescribed for a person addicted to heroin.

Detox is not rehabilitation. It is simply a process to stabilize the body – to clear the system of drugs and/or alcohol – so that rehabilitation can begin.

A More Detailed Explanation of Phase 2: Rehabilitation

Rehabilitation might begin in a 28-, 60- or 90-day treatment facility, as either an "in-patient" (living at the facility) or an "out-patient" (living elsewhere but still spending a great deal of time taking part in activities at a treatment facility). Or, it might be done through a 12-step program, such as AA or NA, or with a therapist trained in addiction, or with one's religious leader, or through a combination of medications and self-help groups or with some mix of these and/or others. It might even be done online – yes, there are online treatment programs.

The components and methods of delivery of an effective rehabilitation program will vary. An addict/alcoholic might find them all at one facility, or they might seek various professionals, such as a trained addictions specialist therapist, a nutritionist, a yoga instructor, a trainer or a sleep specialist. Overall, the objectives of rehabilitation include:

Objectives of Rehabilitation:

- *Brain and Body Healing Activities*
- *Coping Skills Strategies*
- *Dual Diagnosis Treatment (if applicable)*
- *Prescribed Medications (if applicable)*
- *Mindfulness Activities*
- *Therapies*
- *A Strong Family-help Program*

Brain and Body Healing Activities. These are methods for improving the health of the mechanics of neural networks and to repair the physical damage caused by the addiction. We've known for decades the importance of diet, exercise and sleep to the body, but scientific studies of the brain now show how a nutritionally balanced diet, regular exercise and adequate sleep are critical to brain health, as well. (See Chapter 11 for more details.)

Coping Skills Strategies. Your loved one's healthy coping skills have been compromised – compromised by the neural networks they wired in response to one or more of their risk factors (genetics, social environment, childhood trauma, early use and/or mental illness) and/or to the characteristics of their disease (cravings, loss of control, physical dependence and tolerance).

Over time, their healthy coping skills were replaced with the key to their addiction – alcohol or drugs. So their objective now is two-fold: 1) to stop their automatic response (coping skill) to drink or use when cued by the "stuff" of life, and 2) to work on the cues themselves. This includes resolving, or at least coming to grips with, the underlying issues related to their risk factors (childhood trauma, for example), as well as the resulting life problems they've caused by using drugs or alcohol to cope (credit, financial or relationship problems; feelings of shame, fear and anger; an extended period of unemployment, for example).

LOVED ONE IN TREATMENT? NOW WHAT!

Early Recovery

It takes about one year in early recovery for the brain to start to repair (recall Image 3.2 in Chapter 3). It can take up to three years for the addict/alcoholic's new neural networks to embed

> Early recovery takes about one year.

and become second nature. This is not to say addicts/alcoholics won't start enjoying life and making huge strides in their recovery from the beginning. But you have to understand – recovery takes time. Recognizing this fact will help family members and friends, as well as the addict/alcoholic, not to expect that "all is well" as soon as the substance use has stopped.

Additionally, it is not uncommon for people in early treatment to want desperately to abandon their treatment facility or other treatment efforts. They are often afraid. They have not been substance-free in a very long time and are confused by everything that is going on. Here are some of the more common arguments they might try in hopes of getting you to go along with letting them stop or believe their plea that "*this* time really will be different, I promise":

- The kids need me.
- I miss you. I miss my friends.
- I might lose my job.
- The food here stinks.
- I'm not like these people.
- How could you stick me in a place like this? I only have a bed and a nightstand!
- I'm not going to talk about my stuff with a bunch of strangers.
- I don't like my therapist. You should have heard what he told me to do!
- I promise I won't touch alcohol/drugs – ever! I know what I have to do. Just let me come home. Please!
- And, usually the most effective and devastating, "If you love me, you'll let me come home."

> One husband said, "She made it sound like there were bars on the windows and a lock-down at night. She pleaded with me to let her come home. I didn't know what to do, and the kids were crying to me, asking, 'Where's mommy? Where's mommy?'"

It will be very important that you <u>do not give in</u> and that you <u>don't take to heart what they say</u>. Sure, they may feel and/or believe it's awful, and yes, it is different than the way they've been living recently. But letting them return to their routine environment before they've even begun to treat their brain disease probably will not work. Just know, there are no bars on the windows and they cannot be held against their will.

One caveat: Some programs, particularly "boot camp" approaches for changing the behavior of teenagers, have the potential to be abusive. But you have probably screened out such programs prior to your loved one beginning rehab – so complaints about lousy food or conditions by alcoholics/addicts are usually just a way to avoid confronting their disease and are not based in reality. Of course, if you do have any real concerns about possible abuse in a program, do not ignore them and take steps to investigate and/or remove your loved one from the situation.

Dual Diagnosis Treatment. If your loved one suffers from a mental illness and an addiction, it will be important that both be treated at the same time, preferably by the same treatment team (when care is being provided at a treatment facility). As you may have read under "Mental Health Illness," one of the risk factors described in Chapter 7, addicts/alcoholics often turn to their substance of choice as a way of self-medicating their mental illness. If the substance is removed but the mental illness is not treated, their chances of relapse increase significantly. The same is true if the mental illness is treated but the substance misuse continues. The treatment provider needs to help the patient understand their addiction, their mental illness and the impact one has had on the other.[54]

The National Alliance of Mental Illness (NAMI) offers excellent, free self-help programs. Visit www.nami.org for information and locations in your community.

SAMHSA's Mental Health Services Locator

http://mentalhealth.samhsa.gov/databases/

The Substance Abuse and Mental Health Services Administration (SAMHSA) of the U.S. Department of Health and Human Services offers a Locator database with comprehensive information about mental health services and resources in the United States.

Prescription Medications. There is a great deal of debate within addiction circles about using some of the new medications to help with addiction treatment. You may recall reading earlier that an addiction craving can be five times stronger than hardwired, instinctual cravings, such as those that drive us to eat when hungry.

Supervised use of a prescribed medication to help with the addiction cravings can help a person focus on the behavioral changes – the rewiring of neural networks they'll need in order to manage their cues and the underlying behavioral/psychological triggers.

The newer medications used to help with alcohol addiction include Naltrexon (Revia), approved by the FDA in 1994, with an injectable product version (Vivitrol) approved in 2006, and Acamprosate (Campral), approved in 2004.

Medications used to help with treatments of opiate addiction include methadone, buprenorphine and naltrexone (Trexan). At this time, there are no medications to help with stimulant addictions, such as cocaine.[55]

Know that a loved one might also be prescribed medications for a mental illness to help him/her with their dual diagnosis recovery.

"I'd been through three other treatment programs before I heard this about the brain and neural networks and all. For the first time, I understand...," said an alcoholic in rehab.

<u>Mindfulness Activities</u>. By the time an addict/alcoholic enters treatment, their thoughts are consumed 24/7 with "all-things addiction." Just about everything is a cue or trigger and the web of entangled lies and self-deception to keep it all going is massive. Therefore, activities that focus on mindfulness can help with the process of rewiring, changing and developing of new neural networks.

Mindfulness refers not only to moments of being quiet or meditating, but more importantly, to being aware and conscious of the present. Trying to avoid pain, relive the past or postpone the future is what makes an addict/alcoholic's "thinking" go squirrely. Squirrely thoughts trigger using or drinking because drinking or using was how they coped with squirrely thoughts. (A more "scientific" explanation of this concept is presented in later chapters.)

Mindfulness activities should start out small – just five minutes, because it's difficult to go longer (being "really" mindful, that is). These activities basically include anything that helps a person to stay present and to "kick-start" dopamine production in order to find pleasure in the every day "stuff." Mindfulness activities also help a person "buy time" in order to separate emotions from facts and to recognize emotions for what they are so they can be dealt with effectively. This whole concept is explained in more detail in Chapter 11. For now, it is important to understand that mindfulness activities can help an addict/alcoholic develop coping skills and ways to have fun that do not involve alcohol or drugs.

Mindfulness activities include yoga, exercise, spiritual and/or religious practices, meditation, gardening, reading a book, taking up a new hobby, going on a walk and leaving the cell phone behind or doing volunteer work. Anything that grabs one's attention to focus on a particular activity – even if it's just for five minutes – works. As stated, these activities help addicts/alcoholics fight their cues/triggers. Soon these kinds of activities will become critical for recovery – *living* a joy-filled life. Mindfulness activities are all about pushing the brain to develop new neural networks and not slide down the old, embedded thought pathways.

Applying This Research to the First Three Steps of AA and NA

Because the majority of addicts/alcoholics are introduced to and/or use Alcoholics Anonymous (AA) or Narcotics Anonymous (NA) at some point in their treatment and/or recovery, it is helpful to talk about the first three steps of these programs (listed below). Many addicts/alcoholics in early treatment/recovery (and often their family members/friends, as well) are not convinced there is a God or Higher Power, nor do they believe that turning their lives and wills over to one makes any sense. Even though newcomers are assured that their God or Higher Power can be whatever/whomever they so choose, as long as it is something greater than themselves, many report feeling conflicted when they contemplate the first three steps of NA or AA. Here are those steps:

1 - We admitted we were powerless over alcohol/our addiction – that our lives had become unmanageable.

2 - Came to believe that a Power greater than ourselves could restore us to sanity.

3 - Made a decision to turn our will and our lives over to the care of God as we understood God.

For those who are confused by or worried about the meaning of these first three steps, it can help to think of them in terms of the new brain and addiction-related research as described in the following adaptations:

1 - Came to understand the disease of addition as a chronic, often relapsing brain disease, and to accept that I have the disease.

2 - Given the power of addiction cravings and the chemical and structural changes that have occurred in my brain because of my disease and/or my risk factors, I accept that my way of "handling" it by trying to control how much I use or drink cannot work.

3 - Accepting that "my way" did not and cannot work, I know I must abstain from my substance entirely, and I am open to trying any of the various treatment components/options available. If one fails, I will try another.

Sometimes using a concept of the first three steps in this manner can help addicts/alcoholics (and their family members/friends) embrace the notion and benefits of treatment and recovery, even if they do not believe in and/or grasp the 12-step explanation of God or a Higher Power.

Therapies. Various therapies can help addicts/alcoholics come to terms with their underlying triggers, which are often rooted in their risk factors (such as childhood trauma or mental illness), as well as the problems caused by the years of addiction (such as financial, legal, employment and/or relationships problems). Some of the various types of therapies[56] include:

• cognitive-behavioral therapy (CBT), which is aimed at changing the addict/ alcoholic's thoughts about and reactions to relapse-provoking situations and triggers (i.e., rewiring new neural networks for new, healthy coping skills]

• marital, family and couples therapy, which may not occur for several months after treatment begins in order to give all concerned time to come to terms with what has happened and to allow time for everyone to start changing their neural networked thinking and coping patterns

• individual therapy, which is working one-on-one with a therapist

Regardless of the therapy type, it is critical to use a therapist who understands addiction, a specialization for which many therapists (and medical professionals, for that matter) are not trained.

• group therapy, which is generally a group of addict/alcoholics meeting together with a facilitator who is either a therapist, an addiction specialist or an addict/ alcoholic who is further along in his/her recovery

• brief therapies, which are generally one to six sessions designed to promote recognition of the problem and a willingness to change and engage in treatment.

A Strong Family-Help Program. The remaining chapters explain the ways in which family members and friends have been impacted by secondhand drinking/ drugging, particularly in the ways *their* brains have wired neural networks to cope. So as not to be repetitive, the details will not be explained, here. However it is important to recognize that the family members and friends must also receive help. This might be a program at a treatment center or it might be an independent family-help program or it might be some combination of the suggestions offered in Chapters 11-12. Without help targeted to secondhand drinking/drugging impacts, family members and friends will have a more difficult time healing their *brains*, which in turn will not only complicate their lives, but the recovery of their addict/ alcoholic loved ones, as well.

It might help to think of this last statement in terms of a dance. If one partner changes the music or the steps, the "dance" changes. If the other partner does not learn the new music or steps, they will trip on their partner's toes. Additionally, if they do not learn the new steps and their partner is tired of having their toes trodden, the dance may end. Unfortunately, by not learning the new steps or music, that person will probably go on to find another partner who knows their dance. In other words, they'll likely find another alcoholic/addict or someone with similar behaviors. And the same holds true if the family member or friend changes their dance, but the alcoholic/addict does not. Again, this *will* make sense as you read the remaining chapters.

SAMHSA's Substance Abuse Treatment Facility Locator

http://dasis3.samhsa.gov/

This Locator (different from the previous Mental Health Services Locator) provides an on-line resource for finding drug and alcohol abuse treatment programs in the United States. It is updated annually. Here is a sample of the questions for which you can find answers:

- Where can a person with no money and no insurance get treatment?

- What can be done for a family member who needs treatment but refuses to get it or leaves treatment before it is completed?

- What facilities accept court-ordered clients?

- How can I find a facility that specializes in treating abuse of a particular drug (e.g., cocaine, inhalants, etc.)?

- Can you recommend a particular treatment program in my area?

Important: It must be understood that not all addicts/alcoholics need go through a formal treatment program (referring to a 28-day residential or a 90-day intensive outpatient type program, for example) in order to recover. Not all can afford nor do they need such a program, and not everyone is open to it. Regardless of the methods chosen – residential, 12-step, outpatient, addictions specialist therapist, etc., – the objective remains the same: follow a disease management approach that involves detox/stabilization, rehabilitation and continuing care.

A More Detailed Explanation of Phase 3: Continuing Care

Because addiction is a brain disease, it is highly unlikely that all aspects of healing the brain can be completed in 10, 28 or even 60 days. Yes, a great start can be made, but a continuing care (a.k.a. an after care) plan that extends "treatment" for at least a full year is critical. This is not to be confused with being "in treatment" at a facility.

A continuing care plan is a specific strategy that outlines how the addict/alcoholic is going to maintain abstinence *and* a joy-filled life after the detox/stabilization and rehabilitation phases have been completed. Think of it as relapse prevention. And, "What does *this* mean?"

The addict/alcoholic's embedded addiction-related neural networks will be triggered by any number of cues – sound, sight, memory, the

> *Think of continuing care as a relapse prevention plan.*

smell of alcohol, an emotion, a stressful person or situation. Therefore, planning how to prevent and/or handle such cues is critical. Let's face it, treatment for a heart disease patient or diabetic doesn't stop after the person is stabilized, nor is it assumed a patient's diabetes or heart disease goes away after the rehabilitation effort. Instead, those patients are counseled, provided education and behavioral modification strategies, and then they are given a continuing care plan and follow-up with further modifications, if necessary. This same approach must be used with treating addiction. For as you can imagine by now, healing, developing and changing neural networks takes time.

As with rehabilitation, there are a wide range of opportunities and options to include in a continuing care plan. These might include:
• identifying triggers – drug/alcohol-related people, places, things and what to do when confronted with them

• plans/strategies for how to continue improving the health of neural networks (nutrition, exercise, sleep, mindfulness activities)

• drug testing or monitoring programs (sometimes just knowing that random drug tests will occur can keep a person from using or drinking, and the only way an addict/alcoholic can change their brains is to stay substance free)

• assistance in finding financial advisors, medical professionals, addiction therapists in one's home community (actually dealing with the credit crisis, for example)

• scheduling 12-step meeting times and an attendance plan

• working with a sponsor through a 12-step program or finding a mentor or religious advisor to call on

• mindfulness and/or spiritual support activities

• plans for how to handle cravings

• participation in group therapy or other self-help group-type programs

• identifying job-hunting services, parenting classes or legal services

• regular follow-up calls with a peer, monitoring service or treatment center professional.

> **Note:** if the loved one is returning home, family members and/or friends must be part of the decisions concerning conditions and boundaries (more fully explained in Chapters 11 and 12), such as curfews, help with chores, access to the car, substance-use monitoring and what modifications to the plan will be implemented if agreements are violated.

A continuing care plan is most effective if written and signed in the form of a contract, with planned modifications that will "kick-in" if the plan is not followed and/or conditions/boundaries are not met. An example of a boundary with modification scenario might be:
- The family member or friend gets "nervous" when the addict/alcoholic starts acting "funny."

- In the continuing care plan, both "sides" have agreed that if this happens, the family member does not have to "prove" it, nor does the addict/alcoholic have to "defend" against it, rather the family member says something like, "We need to talk." This would have been the agreed upon "code word or phrase" (see text box below) that a meeting with a neutral third-party was needed (someone whom they both would have agreed to be acceptable, such as an addictions specialist therapist or religious leader).

- The neutral third-party then helps them work through what happened.

Part of any continuing care plan should be a weekly, bi-weekly or monthly meeting to evaluate how things are going – preferably in the company of a trained professional who can help with communication so all concerned do not fall into old communication patterns of, "Yeah, but…," or "You said _____." (Chapters 11 and 12 cover this issue more fully.) If addicts/alcoholics are on their own or not affiliated with a treatment center, they may elect to sign-up with a continuing-care specialist or service, someone who calls to verify that all is going according to plan and/or to help with plan revisions if necessary. Some addicts/alcoholics will do their version of a continuing care plan with their AA or NA sponsor, mentor, therapist or spiritual advisor. The important thing is not to assume that once rehab is over a person is "cured."

Include a Code Word or Phrase

It can be very helpful to decide on a code word or phrase, such as, "Can't go there," and include it in a continuing care plan agreement that involves family members or friends. Either party may use the word or phrase to stop a conflict from escalating without having to resolve the conflict or admit guilt. In essence, the code word or phrase "says," "I'm feeling squirrely and don't know how to do this 'right.' I know that what I'm doing is not helpful. This is not an admission of right or wrong. So for now, let's walk away, and I'll put it on the list for things to discuss in our weekly meeting."

One more statement while on this subject: establishing a continuing care plan will not cause an addict/alcoholic who is "in recovery" to relapse. In fact, it can actually help because the more clear

Insisting on a continuing care plan will not cause an addict/alcoholic "in recovery" to relapse.

the boundaries, the less all concerned will get caught up in worrying about the "What if's?" Note the words, "in recovery," however. Being "in recovery" means actively working to stay drug free/sober AND live a joy-filled life.

As daunting as all of this may sound, treatment really can and does work – especially when you leave your loved one's treatment up to *them*. This does not mean you cannot express your concerns, fears, needs and the like, but it's *how* you express yourself that will determine how effective you are. The "how" will make more sense as you understand the impacts secondhand drinking/drugging has had on *your* neural networks. These concepts are the focus of the next several chapters.

Additional Terms You May Hear In Treatment Circles

Boundaries - a term that basically refers to a point or "line" beyond which a certain behavior will trigger a consequence and then actually following through with the stated consequence (in other words, not allowing an excuse to move the boundary). An example of a boundary is for everyone to agree that the addict/alcoholic will not get a car until s/he has a job. If the addict/alcoholic argues a few weeks later that s/he cannot look for a job without a car, it is important not to go along with that argument. Most job applications begin online, and there are always bus lines, cabs, bikes, walking, trains and phones for making other transportation arrangements. To give in after everyone has agreed to the boundary of "no job/no car" is not helpful to the addict/alcoholic trying to recover. It only triggers and/or re-enforces the addict/alcoholic's embedded neural networks that were so effective in getting a family member or friend to go along with their promise that *this* time (I used or drank) was the last time, "I promise."

Family Therapist – often treatment facilities provide a therapist to work with the family members of the client addict/alcoholic. It is important to use this individual to help you understand what is going on and to facilitate conversations with your loved one about matters of concern to you. In early recovery, communication is still very broken – still based on the "addiction ways" of talking – which is why using a family therapist can be especially helpful.

IOP (Intensive Out Patient) – is when clients live at home or in an SLE (sober living environment, see definition below) but they visit the treatment center facility for either day or evening treatment and recovery programs.

Psychosocial Assessment - a questionnaire-type assessment conducted by a clinician to determine a patient's biological, psychological and social experiences/history at the time of admittance to a treatment facility. It is sometimes called a BioPsychoSocial Assessment.

Recovery - addicts/alcoholics who continue to work on treating their addictions after they have stopped their substance use are referred to as being "in recovery." This includes activities such as: going to AA or NA meetings, continuing therapy with an addictions specialist therapist, following a nutritionally healthy diet and/or an exercise program and/or dealing with the fall-out of their addiction (such as repairing credit, searching for a job, handling relationship problems). Addicts/alcoholics in recovery recognize that addiction is not acute, thus addiction treatment cannot be a one-shot effort.

SLE (Sober Living Environment) – is basically a "home" where no alcohol, drugs or paraphernalia are allowed. Often family members and friends are not ready to have the addict/alcoholic move home, or the addict/alcoholic is not ready to move home because of too many triggers or an unhealthy recovery environment. In these instances, a sober living environment home is suggested. You can find these homes in the yellow pages or by contacting a treatment center near you.

Checking items off the list...

✔ **Learn what to look for in and expect from addiction treatment and recovery.**

Points to Remember:

- There is no "one size fits all" model of addiction treatment, however effective addiction treatment should follow the disease management approach and include: 1) detox/stabilization, 2) rehabilitation and 3) continuing care.

- Being in treatment and being in recovery are two different things. Treatment is generally an acute period of time in which the substance use ends, understandings of the disease and repairing of neural networks begins and a continuing care plan is developed and implemented. Recovery means continuing to stay drug free/sober AND live a joy-filled life.

- Having a detailed, written continuing care plan is very important for recovery, especially for an addict/alcoholic who is moving back to the family home.

- Family members and friends have a "right" to say what it is they need and expect. This will not cause a loved one to relapse, although s/he may try to make you feel that way.

- Using a treatment professional, an addiction specialist consultant or therapist to "broker" some of the exchanges among family members early in the treatment process (such as negotiations surrounding the development of a written continuing care plan or talking about what has happened) can be especially helpful.

- Treatment and recovery take time. Your loved one is having to unravel their addiction-related embedded neural networks (with all of their thoughts and behaviors centered on needing and wanting to drink or use and then trying not to) as their coping reaction for just about everything in their lives. A full, happy, joy-filled life is absolutely possible, however. Life with your loved one can be "normal."

CHAPTER 9

How Secondhand Drinking/Drugging Affects the Lives – and Brains – of Family Members and Friends

Imagine carrying on with your plans for the evening, even if your loved one didn't show up and you suspect s/he stopped for a drink. Think about the possibility of going to work with a calm mind – even though your loved one came home loaded the night before and started in on a rant about your not calling the bank to handle the delinquent mortgage payment.

Now picture this: When you feel that sick feeling in your gut or have tortured yourself with worry about what your loved one is "really" up to and want to start peppering him or her with questions about their whereabouts, what if you could simply stop yourself, and say, "Wait! I can't have a logical, thoughtful conversation with a person whose brain disease twists their thinking and makes logic and reasoning just about impossible. I'm not even going to try!"

Perhaps best of all, imagine that you truly do not worry about your loved one's treatment or recovery!

The remaining chapters offer information, followed by suggestions, that can help make these imagined situations your realities. But first, it's helpful to understand the secondhand drinking/drugging impacts you may have experienced. This in turn can help you better understand what experiencing those effects has done to you, and from there, how to "fix it" so that you feel better in spite of the situation and regardless of what your loved one does or doesn't do.

Assessing Your Secondhand Drinking/Drugging Impacts

The impacts of secondhand drinking/drugging on family members and friends are profound. But these impacts are little understood and rarely recognized by society and therefore by the family members and friends, themselves. The following questions[57] provide an informal assessment to get you started. You may have had some of the experiences listed below, or you may have experienced far worse or not as bad. Or you may even be wondering what any of this is about and what it has to do with you.

If you were not fully aware of your loved one's substance misuse, try to think back to any changes in his or her behavior that you can recall (for example, surliness, mood swings, odd hours, disregard for family rules and/or common respect, etc.). Then jot down your thoughts about and reactions to those behavioral changes.

As stated throughout this book, you can use the space below and/or the margins for your answers, or write them on a separate piece of paper.

• Has your loved one's substance misuse caused any of the following problems for you or your family? Please check all that apply:

____ s/he got a DUI or was arrested for _____ , which meant the family's income had to be diverted to help pay fees and fines and you had to take over their driving or "cover" while s/he served jail time or

_____

____ s/he lost a job as a result of substance misuse behaviors, and you've had to _____

____ s/he has incurred high credit card debt, not paid the mortgage, taxes, medical bills, etc., and/or incurred such debt you are now facing bankruptcy and you've had to _____

____ you or your children have experienced verbal, physical or emotional abuse when your loved one misuses or is recovering from a binge or feels guilty and wants you to "forgive" him/her and gets angry when you don't

____ your loved one generally blamed you, your children or someone/something else as the cause of his/her substance misuse and would come at you with twisted, irrational arguments to justify blaming you (and you tried to defend yourself by arguing back)

____ you have lost or had to let go of friendships or family members who refuse to have anything to do with your loved one because of his/her substance misuse behaviors

____ you or your children have become fearful or anxious or depressed because you never know what to expect

____ your worry or fear about the situation gets in the way of your ability to concentrate at work (or your child to concentrate at school)

____ you've found you've changed – you're not the parent or person you want to be because of all the worry, broken promises, frustration, fighting and…

____ you or your children have trouble sleeping well due to worry or fear about "What if _____?"

____ your ability to find joy in the things you used to enjoy has been affected

____ you or your children hate that you have to try cover for your loved one's substance misuse but feel you must do it, anyway

____ you feel embarrassed in your community or with your friends and family because of what they know or have seen of your loved one's substance misuse behaviors

___ you feel your loved one's inability to stop/control their drinking/drugging is a reflection on you – that you and/or your children are not important enough for him/her to want to stop

___ you and your children try and hide how bad it is or make excuses for your loved one's substance misuse behaviors to each other and/or to others

___ you've had to do all the things your loved one no longer does because s/he passes out or it's just easier not to ask, in addition to everything you already do

___ you have increased your own substance use by trying to keep up with your loved one or feeling "Why not?! S/he does it, I might as well, too!" or you find it helps relieve the stress of the situation

___ you've cut back on your own activities in order to keep your children safe or to try and control how much your loved one drinks/uses by being with him/her as much as you can

___ you wish you could just leave

- Have you or other family members tried to get your loved one to stop his/her substance misuse? If yes, please check all that apply:
___ myself – think about what you've tried and how long you've tried

___ children – think about what they've tried and how long they've tried

___ parents – think about what they've tried and how long they've tried

___ friends – think about what they've tried and how long they've tried

___ coworkers – think about what they've tried and how long they've tried

___ others – think about what they've tried and how long they've tried

- Have you ever considered or gotten help for yourself or your children? ___Y ___N If no, did something stop you from doing so, such as you: ___ didn't know where to go for help ___ were worried your loved one would find out ___ thought you should be able to handle it ___ other

- Do you find yourself trying to be all things to all people – especially your children – almost as if you were trying to make up for their having to experience the impacts of secondhand drinking/drugging?

- How are you feeling at this time? ___ hopeful ___ scared ___ not sure ___ angry ___ confused ___ don't really care ___ other

- Are there any specific problems with which you know you'll need help (for instance, dealing with finances, opening communication between addict/alcoholic and child, repairing credit, explaining all of this to close relatives and/or friends, etc.)?

- What are your biggest fears (for example, are you afraid treatment won't work, worried about what will happen after treatment, worried about money, worried about your children, worried about what to tell people)?

• Is there anything else you would like to know or better understand based on what you have read/learned so far?

Understanding How Secondhand Drinking/Drugging Affects the Brain of a Family Member or Friend

As you can imagine, coping with secondhand drinking/drugging has an effect on a family member and/or friend's brain. It has to. Our brains control everything we think, feel, say and do.

But how? What kind of an effect? Family members and friends aren't drinking or using drugs, causing chemical or structural changes in their brains. And nothing about being impacted by someone's substance misuse behaviors sounds like it could result in a brain disease. So where's the connection?

The connection between what happens to the brains of addicts/alcoholics and the brains of their family members/friends comes down to two words: brain maps. In the case of addicts/alcoholics, their brain maps center on their *substance misuse*.

Secondhand drinking/drugging has an affect on the brains of the people who must cope with it.

The brain maps of family members/friends, however, center on their *coping with their loved one's substance misuse behaviors*. And depending on how those brain maps are wired, the neural networks that family members/friends use to deal with their loved one's substance misuse behaviors may or may not be healthy for them.

Here is what can happen to the brain of a family member or friend who repeatedly experiences the effects of secondhand drinking/drugging.

As you recall, the onset of the brain changes for addicts/alcoholics begins when drugs or alcohol start "kicking and kicking and kicking" the pleasure/reward neural networks in the Limbic System (that is, the *dopamine neural networks*). For the majority of family members and friends, the start of the changes to their brains begins with the "kicking and kicking and kicking" of the *fight-or-flight neural networks*, also in the Limbic System.

The fight-or-flight system is also known as the body's stress response system. For the typical family member or friend, living with an addict/alcoholic causes stress. Lots of stress.

Dr. John J. Ratey writes in his book, *SPARK, The Revolutionary New Science of Exercise and the Brain*, "stress is a threat to the body's equilibrium. It's a challenge to react, a call to adapt."[58] Stress can be good, such as planning a wedding, and bad, such as living with an addict/alcoholic.

In a nutshell: the addicts/alcoholics' pleasure/reward neural networks are hijacked, while the family member/friends' fight-or-flight neural networks are hijacked. Both are in the Limbic System, the "reactionary" part of our brain; not in the Cerebral Cortex, the "thinking" part of our brain.

Like the pleasure/reward system, the fight-or-flight system is another instinctual neural network system. Its purpose is to keep us safe and to fleetingly override the "thinking" parts of the brain in order to do so. This instinctual system is what pushes us to "get the heck out of the way" when faced with danger (stress) instead of stopping to rationally "think it through" before reacting. The classic illustration to explain this instinctual system is the image of the caveman who had to either "fight" a great wooly mammoth or take "flight" from it, in order to stay alive. While most of us do not have to face dangerous animals today, our brains retain the fight-or-flight instinct to protect us from danger.

The Fight-or-Flight (a.ka. Stress Response) System

The fight-or-flight system is complex, but in very GENERAL terms, it works as follows.

The system engages when the key stress hormones – adrenaline (epinephrine) and cortisol are triggered. These stress hormones cause a number of reactions: blood vessels under the skin to constrict to prevent blood loss in case of injury; endorphins to kick in to blunt pain; the digestive system to shut down and muscles controlling the bladder to relax in order to conserve glucose.[59] These stress hormones also cause the bronchial tubes of the lungs to dilate in order to carry more oxygen to the muscles; the liver to breakdown stored complex carbohydrates into usable glucose for energy; the blockage of insulin receptors at the nonessential tissues and organ sites in order to increase the flow of glucose to areas needed for fight-or-flight[60] and an increase in heart rate and blood flow to the large muscles so as to enable a person to "run faster, jump higher." This response system even causes the pupils to dilate in order to see better. It's impressive what our bodies can do in such a short time without consciously "thinking" about it!

All of this occurs because the instinctual hardwiring of our fight-or-flight system was "built in" to be triggered by physical danger in order to keep humans safe – "RUN or FIGHT but don't just stand there!! That's a gigantic woolly mammoth coming at you!"

Today, however, *the fight-or-flight system is triggered more often than not by thoughts and emotions rather than actual physical danger.*[61] Nevertheless, all of the physical changes that the system sets in motion – the increased glucose, heart rate and muscle contractions, for example – still occur. Yet, for the most part, a person does not engage in the physical activity that expends the energy these physical changes are meant to support.

"Ever since his suspension from school for drinking at the football game, I'm on pins and needles the whole time he's out with his friends. I try calling the other moms with some kind of off-hand question to see if they know what they're up to. And, then when he gets home, I try to smell his breath, which is pretty hard to do given he won't even hug me, anymore. It's like my heart is racing, non-stop. And, I practically jump out of my skin when the phone rings."

Therefore, if a person is under repeated or constant stress, all of the physiological reactions just "sit" in various body tissues until (or if) they are reabsorbed or expended. The physical and/or emotional health ramifications of chronically activating the fight-or-flight system, but not carrying it through to its conclusion, are many. They may include: headaches, upset stomach, skin rashes, hair loss, racing heartbeat, back pain, muscle aches, anxiety, depression, migraines, difficulty concentrating, vertigo and the like.

A Closer Look at Stress and the Fight-or-Flight Reaction

Complicating this whole process for humans is the fact that, unlike animals, humans do not need obvious danger to activate the fight-or-flight/stress response system. Humans can do this by anticipating, remembering and/or conceptualizing the danger.[62] Quoting Dr. Ratey, again,

> "...We don't have to run from lions, but we're stuck with the instinct....
> The way you choose to cope with stress can change not only how you
> feel, but also how it transforms the brain.... Like most psychiatric issues,
> chronic stress results from the brain getting locked into the same pattern,
> typically one marked by pessimism, fear and retreat. Active coping moves
> you out of this retreat."[63]

What does "active coping" mean? How can we transform the brain by the way we "choose to cope with stress?" How can we have a "choice" over an instinctual reaction?

These are valid questions, but try picturing it this way: In "active coping," the "thinking" part of the brain (the neural networks in the Cerebral Cortex) tells the "reactionary" part of the brain (the neural networks in the Limbic System) to "relax" or "back down" – there's really nothing life-threatening going on. In other words, the "fact of the matter" is not what your "fear of the matter" told you it was. In his book, Dr. Ratey provides a wonderful, illustrative phrase for this concept: "Don't worry, it's a stick, not a snake."[64]

So what are the triggers, the cues, of this system?

Generally, it is an emotion (a feeling), such as fear, anxiety, anger or anticipation.

For the most part, emotions are unconscious, sudden physiological reactions to threat or opportunity [i.e., good and bad stress], and they act as a cue to trigger neural networks to develop adaptive behaviors – such as fear prompting flight from danger or disgust prompting aversion.[65] Emotions are the brain's "way" of pushing us away from danger towards pleasure/reward.[66] The processing of emotions occurs in the Limbic System. Because emotions are what "drive" the actions of our brains, they profoundly affect our decision-making and judgment. Without them, our brains are "like a car with steering but no power."[67]

Emotions contribute to moods. And personality helps shape how a person deals with their emotions and/or moods. Moods are what occur if the emotion-driven brain state continues – whether that is for hours or days or longer in the case of some mental illnesses.[68] Personality (that is, being pessimistic, happy-go-lucky, etc.) is the label assigned to the "mind habits," the patterns of neural network activity a person wires as a result of his/her typical thoughts, feelings and behaviors. Personality is another contributing factor in the mix of how/why a person reacts or responds as they do.

And, the formation of an individual's personality is greatly influenced by learned behaviors –

Several "things" affect if and how we react and respond. They include:

- *Emotions*
- *Moods*
- *Personality*
- *Genetic make-up*
- *Health of the neural networks*
- *Structure of neural networks in the Cerebral Cortex*

However, emotions are of particular importance. They "drive" the actions of our brains and profoundly affect our decision-making and judgment. Without them, our brains are "like a car with steering but no power." (Carter, et al.)

especially as a child – for example, behaviors learned by mimicking a parent or sibling.[69] Personality can be thought of as a "bundle of habitual responses" that become "as much a 'part' of the person as a genetic inclination."[70] And, as is true for the addict/alcoholic (or anyone, for that matter), genetic inclinations (that is, one's genetic makeup) are quite variable and profoundly affect who that particular person "is."

Why a Child's Early Social Environment Plays Such An Important Role

Understanding this last section on how a person's personality is greatly influenced by how s/he learns to perceive the world and behave helps to explain why growing up in a family with active (but undiagnosed, untreated and not effectively discussed) substance abuse/addiction can have such an influence on the wiring of a child's neural networks. The child is mimicking the addict/alcoholic and the non-drinking family member's coping skills and behaviors. This also helps to explain why social environment and childhood trauma are among the key risk factors for developing the disease of addiction.

The last two "things" affecting how we react and respond (in this very general overview) are:

1) The health of our neural networks. This concept was previously mentioned when talking about the brains of addict/alcoholics and will be more fully explained in Chapter 11.

2) How we think, perceive, remember, filter, judge, etc. In other words, how the structure of neural networks in our Cerebral Cortex influence the way we ultimately process the fight-or-flight reactions and visa versa.

All of these factors – personality, mood, emotions, stress response, genetic make-up, health of our neural networks and structure of neural networks in the Cerebral Cortex – weave themselves into the embedded brain maps that direct the way we respond and react to our world. This brings us full circle back to the concept first introduced in Chapter 4, '…everything we think, feel, say and do is governed by how our neural networks wire, and at the same time, our behaviors, thoughts and environment reflect back on our neurons, and influences how they connect.' Talk about cause and effect and effect and cause!

Therefore, as you can imagine, family members or friends who have wired unhealthy coping skills (e.g., rage, retreat, defensiveness, aggressiveness, argumentativeness) in reaction to a loved one's substance misuse behaviors, will also need to work on changing their brains. To change their brains, family members and friends will need to:

1) Develop methods for overriding their unhealthy, embedded fight-or-flight neural networked reactions.

2) Push themselves to "think," to look for the fact behind the emotion in order to develop new neural network responses based on the reasoning capabilities of the Cerebral Cortex.

3) Improve the overall health of their neural networks and overall physical well-being.

You may have correctly concluded by now that the neural networks of alcoholics/addicts are also emotion-driven. However, their "coping skill" was a drug or alcohol. Their work is to rewire how they react to stress (emotions) in ways that do not involve a substance. A family member/friend's work is to rewire how they react to stress (emotions) in ways that do not involve assigning a fact to an emotion and acting on the emotion as if it were fact.

Fear Is a Big One

Fear is one of the most common emotions experienced by family members and friends of a substance abuser, addict or alcoholic, and it generally starts with, "What if _____?"

What if he drinks? What if she tries to pick up the kids when she's drunk? What if he gets busted? What if she gets loud and obnoxious at mom's birthday party? What if my daughter says anything? What if treatment doesn't work?

Entire afternoons can feel like one long, "what if?" because one "what if?" leads to another and that leads to still another. Worrying about "what if" is jam-packed with fear.

So, the next time you hear your inner voice saying, "What if_____?" stop yourself for a minute and try to register your heartbeat (is it racing?), your facial expression (is your brow furrowed, are your lips pursed?), your jaw position (is it

When you feel that anxious, worried feeling, ask yourself, "Is it a stick or a snake?"

clenched?) and your thoughts (are they bouncing over a number of "what if" options?). Any one of these is your signal to stop and ask yourself, "Is this a stick or a snake?"

But then what?

To answer this question, we move on to Chapters 11 and 12. There you will find suggestions for what to do next and guidance for learning how not to react to an emotion as if it were fact. In other words, how not to engage the fight-or-flight /stress response neural network system (or at least shut it down sooner, rather than later).

Checking items off the lists...

✔ **Learn what has happened to you – that is, understand the effects of secondhand drinking/drugging.**

Points to Remember:

- Family members and friends of an addict/alcohol also experience neural network changes, primarily related to the fight-or-flight/stress response system.

- If chronically activated, the fight-or-flight/stress response system can cause physical and/or psychological problems.

- Informally assessing the secondhand drinking/drugging impacts you have experienced can help you better see what you can do to "fix" things and feel better – in spite of the situation and regardless of what your loved one does or doesn't do.

- Understanding the concepts of personality, mood, emotions, stress response, genetic make-up, health of our neural networks and the structure of neural networks in the Cerebral Cortex can further help you make neural network changes that can improve your life.

- When feeling anxious (or stress of any kind), it can help to stop and ask yourself, "Is it a stick or a snake?" (which means, "Is my reaction based on reality or on an imagined fear?") This question is an important, but simple, tool that can help you begin to rewire your own neural networks – the remaining chapters will provide you with others.

CHAPTER 10

Understand the Connection Between Secondhand Drinking/Drugging and Codependency

The term, "codependent," was briefly introduced in the definitions in Chapter 1. You may have seen it in magazines and online articles. Or perhaps you've heard it on TV talk shows. In the world of treatment and recovery, it is used OFTEN, so it is important for you to understand codependency and the connection between it and secondhand drinking/drugging.

"Codependent" is used to describe a person, typically a family member or friend, who is "co" "dependent" with the alcoholic/addict on his or her addiction. Just as the alcoholic/addict is focused (dependent) on finding, seeking, using, recovering from their substance and grappling with the resulting changes in their neural networks, so too have family members and friends' lives been focused (dependent) on trying to get the alcoholic/addict to stop and grappling with the resulting changes in their neural networks. Family members and friends have become co-dependent with the addict/alcoholic on his/her addiction, and in the process, the family member/friend (codependent) adapts to the unacceptable substance misuse behaviors in order to cope (and in some cases, survive). These coping behaviors – adaptations – are called "codependency."

Against the backdrop of this new brain research, we can also think of the term, "codependent," as a label to identify a person who has developed the fight-or-flight/ stress response kinds of neural network reactions and coping patterns (described in Chapter 9) when repeatedly confronted with secondhand drinking/drugging.

All of this helps to explain why addiction is often referred to as a "family disease." All members in the family develop unhealthy neural networks they would not have wired were it not for *Addiction is often referred to as a "family disease."* the undiagnosed, untreated, misunderstood and not effectively discussed disease of addiction.

But first, let's explore the original concept of codependency and how the term/ definition has evolved.

"Codependency" Further Explained

The original concept of codependency was developed to describe the responses and behaviors a person developed from living with an alcoholic or drug addict. Subsequent study found that people living with a chronically physically or mentally ill person also developed similar kinds of emotional responses and behaviors. Today, the term codependent has been broadened to describe a person who grew up and/or lives in a dysfunctional family.[71]

A dysfunctional family is defined as one where one or more of the following underlying problems existed (or exists):

- An addiction by a family member to drugs, alcohol, relationships, work, food, sex or gambling.

- The existence of physical, emotional or sexual abuse.

- The presence of a family member suffering from a chronic mental or physical illness. [72]

And what does all of this have to do with your loved one's addiction and treatment, secondhand drinking/drugging and the coping skills of family members and friends?

First of all, it is important to understand that the mere presence of one of these underlying problems is not what makes a family dysfunctional. What makes it dysfunctional is when a family member's confusion, sadness, fear, anger, pain or shame for the underlying problem is ignored, ridiculed, minimized or denied.[73]

And secondly, it is important to understand the family has to break the denial in order to deal with the problem. For when family members do not openly and honestly acknowledge a problem exists, they most certainly don't talk about it or confront it. Sure, they may yell and scream and rant and rave, but they do not "talk" in a way that effectively leads to change. This leaves each family member to do one or more of the following:
- interpret what *they* think is going on

- obey the family rules at all costs – especially the two primary rules:
    Rule #1 – the alcoholic/addict's drinking/drug abuse is not the issue
    Rule #2 – do not talk to anyone (not family, not friends) about it, and above all, attack, minimize or discredit any family member who does.

- adopt coping skills to suppress their emotions so they don't spill over and break one of the family rules (which in time multiply and are ever changing) – or to make the feeling caused by the emotion go away

- assume their needs and wants are not worthy of attention (since everyone's focus must be on the needs and demands of the family member who is ill or addicted or abusing drugs or alcohol and that to ask for or expect attention is selfish or petty).

The Consequences of Codependency/Secondhand Drinking Drugging

Because there is no open, honest recognition and/or statement of the problem, one family member may try to reason with the alcoholic/addict, while another may learn to "read" the addict/alcoholic's behavior in order to assess what's about to happen and how bad it will be. As a result, this family member often learns to modify his or her own behavior or may try to manipulate the behavior of others in order to pacify the alcoholic/addict and diffuse the situation. A third family member may take it upon him/herself to cover up after the alcoholic/addict's binge, while another may try convince their loved one to stop entirely. One may plead, scream, yell, cry or perfect the silent treatment. And, still another may decide it's too crazy and leave altogether. All of these behaviors are methods family members/friends use to cope with secondhand drinking/drugging.

When people place the health, welfare and safety of others before their own in this manner, they can lose contact with their own needs, desires and sense of self. This can affect their ability to have a healthy and satisfying relationship with family, friends, bosses, fellow-workers and significant others. In fact, codependents often marry alcoholics/addicts. Crazy as it may seem, it's understandable given their inordinately high tolerance for the unacceptable. They may also suffer from chronic anxiety, depression and stress-related medical disorders such as lower back pain, insomnia, high blood pressure, skin rashes and migraines. Some may even drink too much. Some may ultimately restart the cycle by becoming alcoholics/addicts themselves. (You may have identified this pattern in your loved one's life when completing the risk factors assessment in Chapter 7. In other words, your loved one may have grown up in an alcoholic or drug addiction family and that experience may have in turn contributed to his/her own addiction.)

The foregoing is the crux of what happens to family members and friends who must repeatedly deal with a loved one's unacknowledged, untreated, misunderstood disease in order to cope as the dysfunction continues. These neural networks then embed and become the coping skills and thought processes family and friends use in their other relationships, as well – those with co-workers, fellow students, family, friends and even with strangers on the street.

So, now what!?

Assessing Coping Skills Adaptations to Secondhand Drinking/ Drugging Impacts

To better understand the thought processes, coping skills and personality traits you may have adopted, developed or used in order to stay safe in the face of the secondhand drinking/drugging impacts you've experienced, consider answering the following questions.[74] This is an informal assessment/series of questions provided by The Sequoia Center, a Northern California drug and alcohol treatment and recovery center. It is not an "official" evaluation or diagnosis of codependency. However, the insights this kind of an informal assessment can provide will help you better appreciate what you can do to heal your own neural network responses. By changing the neural networks that are harming you and your relationships, you can improve your quality of life and help your addict/alcoholic loved one in recovery – though helping yourself is reason enough!

Answer each question with your first reaction and write down whether your response is: (Y) yes or (N) no or (S) sometimes. (You'll see how to score your assessment at the end.)

1. Is your attention focused on protecting or pleasing others?

2. Are you highly critical of yourself?

3. Does it upset you when people are critical of you?

4. Are you more aware of how others feel than of how you feel?

5. Do you have difficulty saying, "No," when someone asks for your help (even if saying "yes" causes you to overextend yourself)?

6. Does what others think of you affect how you feel about yourself?

7. Do you keep silent to keep the peace and/or avoid arguments?

8. Is it hard for you to express your feelings when someone hurts your feelings?

9. Do you feel guilty when you stand up for yourself instead of giving in to others?

10. Do you or did you live with someone who abused/was addicted to alcohol or drugs or was chronically ill (physically or mentally)?

11. Do you tend not to express your emotions or reactions spontaneously, instead taking your cues for how to express them from others or the situation?

12. Do you try to solve the problems and relieve the pain of those you love and worry their lives would go downhill without your constant efforts?

13. Do you hold onto relationships that aren't working, believing there is something you can or should be doing to make it work?

14. Do you have stress related illnesses (headaches, depression, skin rashes)?

15. Do you work or eat or exercise compulsively?

16. Do you fail to recognize your accomplishments or minimize them when someone else does?

17. Do you fail to give much thought to what you like or where you want to go or what you want to do with your life?

18. Does fear of rejection or criticism affect what you say or do?

19. Do you feel more alive when handling, worrying about and/or doing things for others?

20. Do you take care of others easily yet find it difficult to do something just for yourself?

21. Have you slowly withdrawn from extended family, friends and/or your regular activities over the years?

22. Do you spend a lot of time worrying or anticipating and planning for every possible eventuality of a perceived problem?

23. Do you shut down emotionally when you are in conflict or facing an angry person?

24. Do you often mistrust your own feelings and fret about whether they're acceptable or justified before you express them?

25. Do you try to "read" the words of others in order to determine their "true" feelings instead of taking what they say at face value?

26. Does your life feel chaotic or out of control?

27. Do you feel a need to argue over differences of opinion until the other person sees and/or agrees with your view and feel angry or wrong or sad if they don't?

28. Do you find yourself feeling angry often?

29. Have you lived with someone who belittles or withholds "normal" demonstrations of love and affection?

30. Do you rarely set aside time to do things you want to do, things that are not "productive" or accomplishing something for someone else?

31. Do you have a hard time doing a "good enough" job or do you keep at it until you think it's just about perfect?

32. Do you have trouble asking for help or for what you need, or do you have trouble with even knowing you need help or want something?

33. Do you find yourself trying to do something productive, even juggling several things at once, most of the time?

34. Do you procrastinate?

35. Do you feel humiliation or that you've somehow failed if your child, spouse or significant other makes a mistake or gets into trouble?

36. Are you most comfortable (not necessarily happy, but comfortable) when things are kind of crazy or chaotic or there's lots to do?

To score, each "yes" counts as 1 and each "sometimes" counts as ½. If you scored:

1 – 5	you are probably doing just fine
6 – 12	you may be slightly codependent (meaning affected by secondhand drinking/drugging impacts)
13 – 22	you probably are codependent
23 – 36	it's probably a good thing you're reading this book!

Now, if you are up to it, go back through, and where applicable, jot down the emotion (such as anger, fear, anxiety) and/or personality trait (such as, optimist, procrastinator, pessimist) that comes to mind. For example, with #3, the emotion might be "worried" and/or "anxious." Don't struggle with this effort and don't feel judged by it. Remember, you were coping/surviving something you didn't understand. And besides, not all of your coping skills/personality traits are "bad" (as you'll understand when you read the next section).

The reason for doing this step is to see if you can identify a pattern of emotions and/or personality traits. It may be far too early in the process of trying to understand all of this information for this effort to make sense, let alone do. So, of course, feel free to skip it and return later if you're so inclined.

The results of the assessment, itself, can help make sense of the suggestions offered in Chapters 11 and 12. These chapters deal with how to confront your emotions/personality traits in order to deal with the reality (the fact that it is a stick) instead of the emotion (the fear that it is a snake) and thereby respond accordingly.

Secondhand Drinking/Drugging Coping Skills Are Not All Bad

If you scored high on that last assessment, you're likely having a reaction similar to most family members/friends – "So??? What's wrong with being kind, caring, wanting to make things work out for everyone, deferring to others...?" And, the simple answer is, "Nothing!"

Family members/friends of addicts/alcoholics are some of the nicest, most empathetic, "give the shirt off their back" kinds of people. And, there's nothing wrong with that. But when these gestures are always outwardly directed (like towards your loved ones) in an attempt to get someone else to do something, then *your personal satisfaction slowly becomes contingent on another person's reaction* to your gestures. For example, when your husband/wife does not cut down or stop drinking after all you've done to help them, you might withdraw or get vindictive or convince yourself there must be something more you can do. Or when your child doesn't thank you enough for something you've done, you may feel angry or like a victim – "No matter what I do, it's not good enough."

The objective, now, is to learn how to *re-direct* some of this focus, attention, caring and concern *towards yourself* and to let others take care of themselves. You'll find suggestions on how to do this in the remaining chapters. An additional side benefit of following these suggestions will be helping your loved one BECAUSE you are helping yourself.

Checking items off the list...

✔ **Understand the connection between secondhand drinking/drugging and codependency.**

Points to Remember:
- The term, "codependent," has a long history in the world of addiction treatment and recovery. It is used to describe a person, typically a family member or friend, who has become "co" "dependent" with

an addict/alcoholic on the addict/alcoholic's addiction. It is also used to describe a person raised in a dysfunctional family. Against the backdrop of this new brain research, we can also think of the term as a label to identify a person who has developed fight-or-flight/stress response kinds of neural network reactions and coping patterns (described in Chapter 9) when repeatedly confronted with secondhand drinking/drugging.

• Part of the "cause" of codependency is the denial of the fact that an addiction (or some other "elephant" in the living room) exists and the support of the two unspoken rules in the alcoholic/addict family: 1) our loved one's drugging or drinking is not the problem; 2) we do not talk to anyone (not family, not friends) about this. To cope in this kind of family dynamic, family members embed brain maps for a variety of coping skills, some of which impact that person's health, happiness and sense of self.

• Completing an informal assessment/series of questions to identify coping skills adaptations to secondhand drinking/drugging impacts can be helpful.

CHAPTER 11

Taking Control of Your Life

Likely you are feeling pretty overwhelmed right about now. You've been given a great deal of information in these pages, some of which you may not agree with, understand or connect to your situation. That's normal and certainly okay. Regardless, reading these next two chapters is still worth the effort, and you may find that in a few weeks and/or months this information will nudge at your thoughts, and you'll be able to re-read various sections from a different perspective.

Four Things You Can Do Now, Even If You Do Nothing Else: Nutrition, Exercise, Sleep and Mindfulness Activities for Brain Health

As has been stated throughout this book, a person can change their behaviors by rewiring and improving the health of their neural networks (that is, the neurons, synapses, branchlike extensions, neurotransmitters, receptors and the automatic responses to triggers/cues). To that end, this new brain research is helping us understand that four key activities we've long understood to be good for the physical body are also good for the brain. They are: nutrition, sleep, exercise and mindfulness activities. The following provides an overview with a more detailed explanation of each activity to follow.

But first, a quick review of neurotransmitters. As you read in Chapter 4, neurotransmitters are chemical messengers that float the signal from one neuron's axon (outgoing branchlike extension) across the synapse to bind to receptors on the receiving neuron's dendrite (incoming branchlike extension). To help you better understand the functions of the three most common neurotransmitters you will hear about in the world of treatment and recovery, here is an overview:
• serotonin helps the neural networks that keep brain activity in check, especially that associated with mood, impulsivity, anger and aggressiveness

• norepinephrine helps to amplify signals, especially those associated with attention, perception, motivation and arousal

• dopamine – our "feel good" neurotransmitter, the key to the pleasure/reward neural networks – helps with learning, satisfaction, attention and movement.[75]

While these three neurotransmitters facilitate communication between neurons, there are two other very important neurotransmitters: one that starts the electrical signaling – glutamate, and one that stops it – gammaaminobutryic acid (GABA).

And, not to be outdone!, there is another important piece to the neural network – a group of molecules called neurotrophins. The most prominent of these is BDNF, a molecule that "builds and maintains" the neural network infrastructure. It actually "nourishes neurons like fertilizer."[76] This "bolstering of the infrastructure" is what "allows the new information to stick as a memory." [77] In other words, it is a part of what allows a person to change their brain.

So where does healthy nutrition, adequate sleep, regular exercise and mindfulness activities fit with all of this?

They all contribute to the health and support of these various neurotransmitters and neurotrophins, which in turn support the health of the brain's neural networks. (Exercise, for example, elevates levels of BDNF.[78])

Having the general knowledge of how our brains work gives us incredible power to change them. For addicts/alcoholics, family members and friends, alike, this research can stop the guilt and shame and emotions (feelings) of helplessness, hopelessness and fear that get in the way of a joy-filled life. Now, for a more complete explanation of how and why these four activities are so important to brain health.

A More Detailed Explanation of Nutrition

Unlike other body organs, the brain is incapable of making and storing glucose, which is its sole fuel source. No fuel, no brain activity. The brain requires a daily dose of about twenty percent of the body's glucose supply – a staggering amount given the brain is only two percent of the body's total weight. [79]

The brain gets its glucose supply from the carbohydrates in the foods we eat, which are broken down and transported to the brain via the bloodstream. For optimum brain health, however, it can't be

Think of nutrition as "food" for "thought." The more nutrient-rich the food, the "better" the thought.

any old carbohydrates, like those in candy or sugar-packed soft drinks. The brain needs the complex carbohydrate variety, such as that found in whole grains, fruits and vegetables.

And while glucose is essential, so is protein (like that found in lean meats, poultry, fish, beans, eggs, milk products). Protein serves as "the basic building block of the brain's tissue," AND it helps in the production of neurotransmitters[80] and neurotrophins.

Healthy fats, like omega-3 fatty acids found in tuna and salmon, are important for building the neuron's cell membrane and nerve fiber insulation,[81] as well as "synaptic plasticity" and functions related to memory and learning.[82]

And it goes on and on from there.

Healthy nutrition is astoundingly important to brain health – something only known and understood as a result of the new brain research. But if you are not inclined to learn the nitty-gritty about nutrition, and let's face it, who has the time when grappling with a loved one's addiction and/or treatment, following the U.S. Department of Health and Human Services and U.S. Department of Agriculture's

Dietary Guidelines (visually shown in the Food Pyramid) covers the basics. In a nutshell, these guidelines suggest you:

- emphasize fruits, vegetables, whole grains, and fat-free or low-fat milk and milk products

- include lean meats, poultry, fish, beans, eggs, and nuts

- keep saturated fats, trans fats, cholesterol, salt (sodium) and simple sugars low

- stay within daily calorie needs[83] (yes, excess calories impact brain health – especially the flexibility of the synapses and increased vulnerability to cell damage[84]).

Visit www.mypyramid.gov/guidelines for more information.

A More Detailed Explanation of Exercise

Using a hiking metaphor, in order to change the brain, a person has to let the old, well-worn neural network pathways grow over while s/he slashes and treads a whole new series of trails. Or,

Exercise is as important for our brains as it is for our bodies.

to use a traffic metaphor, a person has to take a different highway to detour around a road closure.

For the family member or friend under the chronic stress of secondhand drinking/drugging impacts (or the addict/alcoholic or anyone else wishing to improve their brain health), exercise can be a brain-saver. It increases levels of serotonin, norepinephrine and dopamine and rebuilds the connections between the billions of neurons in the brain.[85] Mentioned above, exercise increases levels of BDNF. These are the neurotrophins that nourish our brain cells "like fertilizer" and allow "new information to stick as a memory."

Exercise also pumps blood flow and oxygen (the other critical component, in addition to the glucose previously mentioned, necessary to keep the brain alive) to the brain.[86] Further, exercise guards against stress![87] And, it helps to get rid of all that unexpended "stuff" triggered by the fight-or-flight/stress response system. It also helps with the signaling neurotransmitters, GABA and glutamate.

The further specifics of exercise are equally interesting, but in the hopes of not overwhelming you, suffice it to say, it is critical to brain health.

How much does it take? An average of 45 minutes/day is best, but even 15 minutes helps.[88]

A More Detailed Explanation of Sleep

Sleep provides a third kind of critical support for brain health. And, generally all concerned get very little of what is known as "good sleep." Passing out from too much alcohol or drug use or sleeping in fits and starts as a result of too much anxiety and worry is not considered "sleep."

It takes about 6.5 to 8 hours of uninterrupted, peaceful sleep to give the brain what it needs, namely "down time" – not to be confused with idle time. Believe it or not, the brain remains incredibly active during sleep.[89] Sleep allows the brain to repair neurons and sort, process and memorize that day's activities.[90] [91]

A More Detailed Explanation of Mindfulness Activities

By the time a loved one enters (or is seriously contemplating) treatment, all concerned – family members, friends, alcoholics/addicts – are consumed 24/7 with thoughts related to the addiction and/or secondhand drinking/drugging impacts. Mindfulness, then, is about changing neural networks by changing our thoughts.

As you can imagine, it must start out in very small increments. To think about not thinking about anything related to the addiction for an hour is impossible at first. To think about not thinking about the situation for 5 minutes is doable. And actually taking five minutes to engage in a thought-calming process helps people understand that they can let go a little. This "letting go" helps them see that stopping their focus on the addiction and its effects does not lead to the worst case scenario(s) they've imagined would happen.

Mindfulness activities help you with responding vs. reacting.

Reacting = behavior without thinking. Reactions originate in the Limbic System.

Responding = behavior preceded by thinking. Responses originate in the Cerebral Cortex.

As you become comfortable with five minutes, you can move it to 10 and then 20 and then an hour and so-on. Eventually, you really will find yourself stringing together days-at-a-time of calm and joy-filled thoughts, and thereby activities, you'd never imagined were possible.

Mindfulness activities include just about anything that requires a person's focused attention, such as doing yoga, exercising (and keeping your thoughts focused on the physical activity and not on texting or talking on the phone) or a walk (and making yourself notice the colors and sound around you). These activities could also involve reading a book, meditating, engaging in spiritual practices, having fun or learning something entirely new. Mindfulness is about forging a new neural pathway to give your brain a different place from which to think, feel, say and do.

Mindfulness takes practice, but at least you can start with just 5-minute increments at a time.

Coming to Grips With Key Stress Triggers – Understanding the Concepts of "Enabling" and "Boundaries"

Even if individuals are able to immediately improve their nutrition, mindfulness, exercise and sleep patterns (as just described), there may still be a missing piece for family members and friends. That "missing piece" is having an understanding of the concepts of "enabling" and "boundaries." Enabling behaviors

LOVED ONE IN TREATMENT? NOW WHAT!

are what a family member or friend does in order to adapt to the substance misuse behaviors as somehow normal or excusable or something to be hidden. Boundaries are "limits" or consequences one sets and sticks to.

Together, enabling behaviors and poor and/or changing boundaries are two factors that cause people to tolerate the progression of "awfulness" they could not have envisioned in the beginning. They are what allow "denial" (described in Chapter 6) to continue. They are what contribute to the dysfunction in the family. They are what trigger fight-or-flight neural networks, reacting to emotions as if they were fact. Stopping enabling behaviors and setting boundaries is critical to rewiring neural networks.

The following will help you to identify your enabling behaviors and changing boundaries, if you have any. The remainder of this chapter can help you identify ways to change them, if you need to.

<u>Enabling Behaviors</u>
- Beginning with the statement, "I allow my loved one (spouse, child, parent, sibling, friend) who is misusing alcohol and/or drugs to…," check those that apply:
    ___ verbally, emotionally or physically abuse me or my children or other family members

    ___ slide by at work while I cover for him/her

    ___ come and go at all hours

    ___ not spend time with the children or me

    ___ not keep appointments or follow-through with plans

    ___ not repay debts

    ___ be bailed out of jail

    ___ live rent free

    ___ use alcohol or drugs in my home

    ___ borrow money

    ___ have meals prepared or laundry done by me when s/he was/is fully capable of helping and/or doing so

    ___ use my car

    ___ other

    Those you have checked above are examples of enabling behaviors.
- Beginning with the word, "I…," check those that apply:
    ___ protect my loved one from others or protect others from my loved one

    ___ make excuses for my loved one's behaviors

    ___ minimize my loved one's actions, lies and excuses

    ___ don't confront my loved one because of his/her possible reactions

___ lie about what is really going on to myself and others

___ don't confront (at least in a productive manner) my loved one when s/he has broken a promise to me

___ accept my loved one's explanations and reasons for his/her behaviors

___ lend money when I know s/he has not stopped drinking or using

___ pretend to the children that nothing is wrong, that it's not as bad as it seems, or that it's something else

___ other

Those you have checked above are further examples of enabling behaviors.

Signs of Unhealthy Boundaries

As you would guess, engaging in enabling behaviors means there is no healthy boundary.

Setting Boundaries – the Key to Stopping Enabling Behaviors

Setting boundaries is about minding your own business and allowing others to mind theirs. It's about not making another person's problem yours or trying to smooth the way for other people so they do not "suffer."'

A boundary is the "line" that establishes where you and your business leave off and where other people and their business begins. Sounds rather drastic, selfish even!

But it's really not. Minding your own business is about letting other people (including your children) take care of anything and everything that is within their power to do. It's about letting them live *their* lives while you live yours. It's okay to offer a gentle reminder or be willing to help. But it is not okay to butt in, or to manipulate through asking endless variations of the same question in order to get the answer or behavior *you* want, or to nag until other people do what you think is best for them. This includes, by the way, how (or if) the addict/alcoholic chooses treatment and/or recovery.

(Be aware that the following does not explain "how" to set boundaries. Rather it shows you examples of boundary-setting activities and gives you goals to shoot for. The "how" of boundary setting is explained in Chapter 12.)

Types of boundaries a family member or friend might set include:

• not talking about anything important with the alcoholic/addict when s/he is drinking or hung over or anxious about treatment/recovery

• not driving with alcoholics/addicts (they're good at hiding how much they've had to drink/use) until they are solid in their recovery

• cutting back your volunteer hours in your child's classroom, if applicable, to just one afternoon a week instead of two or three to leave time for you to do something you want to do that's not related to helping anyone else

- not having alcohol at family get-togethers (if the alcoholic/addict or family members and friends do not want to come, that's their decision)

- getting help for yourself

- stepping aside; removing the target (namely your reactions) that addicts/ alcoholics try to hit with their blame

- deciding not to engage in pointless arguments ("No." is a complete sentence)

- starting a regular exercise program, regardless of whose crisis erupts as you're getting ready to go – deal with it later

- not visiting an actively drinking alcoholic/addict relative out of a sense of duty or just because the person is your relative

- not returning a phone call message laden with guilt, such as, "You haven't called me today…Where are you?…It must be nice to be so busy…"

- refusing to give any more money to your alcoholic/addict loved one

- requiring other family members to help with chores, driving, shopping and the like (Really, you don't have to do it all; others are capable of doing and helping and may even be grateful to be given the chance. Often it's guilt over what they're going through that causes us want to "make it up to them" by "doing it all" so "at least they don't have to do *that*, too!")

- taking a nap instead of doing one more thing on your list of things to do

- letting the alcoholic/addict take FULL responsibility for ALL of the consequences of his or her actions and inaction

- talking with the alcoholic/addict about his/her drinking/drugging or treatment/ recovery and how it's affecting you (and the children, if applicable) in a way that is not designed to necessarily resolve anything, but to at least start calling it like it is; talking in an honest, non-threatening, non-judgmental manner when s/he has not been drinking/using and without an expectation or demand s/he change or stop.

And now…moving on to how you might start setting these boundaries.

Checking Items Off the List

✔ **Understand key concepts to start taking control of your life.**

Points to Remember:
- Exercise, sleep, nutrition and mindfulness activities are keys to changing and/or improving the health of neural networks. These are changes a person can begin immediately, which in and of themselves will help individuals improve their brain health. That improvement can then set the stage for making other neural network changes, such as coping with an addict/alcoholic's addiction and/or treatment and recovery behaviors. Suggestions for this last part are presented in the next chapter.

- Recognizing two key stress triggers – enabling behaviors (behaviors that excuse the inexcusable as somehow normal or acceptable) and the lack of boundaries – can be key to changing your brain.

CHAPTER 12

Changing Where and How You Think

A life of rampant enabling behaviors and poor boundaries in a family or friendship with an addict/alcoholic results in a life of reactivity, of being on high alert, hyper-vigilant because of the ever-changing landscape of the relationships.

Change for family members and friends, therefore, will require changing *where* and *how* they think – moving from "reacting" to "responding." [Note: the "how" portion of that last statement refers to the perception-, memory- and judgment-types of neural networks in the Cerebral Cortex.]

As stated before, responding allows us to access the "thinking" part of our brain (Cerebral Cortex). Behaviors based on thinking are far more effective than those based on "reacting" (that is, those which follow the flight-or-fight neural pathways in the Limbic System). This switch – from the Limbic System to and within the Cerebral Cortex – is what allows a family member or friend to stop enabling and start setting healthy boundaries.

If you are attempting to make these switches, consider the following suggestions for changing – not *what* you think (you cannot help your initial emotion, an emotion just happens), but *where* and *how* you think. These suggestions are grouped in four general categories:

- Jar Your Thinking
- Change Perspective
- Improve Communication
- Set Boundaries.

You may or may not need to try some of these, or you may not want to try any until you've learned more. For now, just let the concepts register. What you want to do with them will become clear as you learn more and become more comfortable with all of this information.

Suggestions to Help Jar Your Thinking

Stop yourself as soon as you are aware of that surge of emotion – anxiety, fear, sadness, anger – to give yourself a moment to check that the reality (the fact) triggering the emotion is, in fact, what you want to react to. For example, if your child spills some water and you feel anger rising, stopping yourself can give you the moment you need to realize your anger is not at your child and the water, but at something that occurred two nights ago – your loved one drank again, and you've been wandering around in a swirl of thoughts and emotions ever since. The spilled water was just the catalyst.

- Some people wear rubber bands on their wrists, which they immediately snap when feelings of anxiety arise, in order to jar their thinking – to move it from the Limbic System to the Cerebral Cortex.

- Some use a word like THINK or STOP to jar their "thinking" neural networks.

- Some use slogans or sayings – taping them on their car dash, bathroom mirror or desk top – as a reminder of an overall behavior they want to change.

Consider talking to someone else because, unfortunately, your loved one is not going to be there for you. Addicts/alcoholics generally cannot give the kind of apology a family member/friend needs to hear, for example, until they are further along in their own treatment/recovery. It can take months before they can face all they have done to hurt you. Additionally, they will not be able to listen to your feelings and respond in a manner that will help you – again, they are (and need to) work on their own issues. To help you with options for talking to someone else, consider:

- Therapies. Many family members/friends try one or more types of therapies (the same types as the alcoholic/addict might use), including:
    - cognitive-behavioral therapy (CBT), which is aimed at changing the family member/friend's thoughts about and reactions to relapse-provoking situations (i.e., rewiring new neural networks)

    - marital, family and couples therapy (although this often occurs several months after treatment is started to give all concerned time to come to terms with what's gone on and to start the process of changing their brains)

    - individual therapy, which is working one-on-one with a therapist

    - group therapy, which can be meeting with other family members and friends of addicts/alcoholics and a facilitator, who might be an addictions specialist therapist or a family member/friend with more time in recovery

    - brief therapies, which are generally one to six sessions designed to promote recognition of the problem and a willingness to change.

Regardless of which therapy type is pursued, it is critical to use a therapist who understands addiction. Unfortunately, many therapists are not trained in this area.

- 12-step programs. Often family members and friends attend one of the following 12-step programs: Al-Anon, Nar-Anon, Alateen, ACA (Adult Children of Alcoholics) and CoDA (Codependents Anonymous). Looking on the internet or in the yellow pages will give you details on where to call for meeting times and locations.

- Talking with a spiritual advisor and/or following a faith-based program or finding a mentor (all should have an understanding of addiction, by the way).

- National Alliance on Mental Illness (NAMI.org) Family-to-Family program offers help to those whose loved one has a dual diagnosis (and, like a 12-step program, it's free!).

Seek professional advice to help with financial planning, credit recovery, parenting issues, legal matters and to better handle the additional stresses beyond those with which you are already coping.

Suggestions to Help Change Perspective

Change the dial on "self-talk radio," which means to stop those one-sided conversations you have with yourself: "There you go, again." "You're so stupid." "Why'd you say that?" "I should have finished that and would have if I wasn't so disorganized." Now, ask yourself, "Would I ever speak to a friend like that?" Of course not. It is important to stop being so hard on yourself. When you change the channel on "self-talk radio," you can begin to see your many great qualities. And, in time, you will accept the idea that you are a person with feelings who deserves the respect of others, not only from your alcoholic/addict loved one, but also from yourself.

Banish absolutes – all good/all bad, all right/all wrong. Generally people and situations are not "all" of anything. Stopping yourself from reacting to the emotions triggered by your loved one's rotten substance misuse behaviors, for example, helps you recognize that not ALL of their behaviors are rotten. When you stop those all-or-nothing reactions, you can love him/her with your heart and not your head. You can come to accept that at his/her core, s/he is a good person with a chronic, often relapsing brain disease that has affected his/her thinking and behaviors. Note: This is not to say you have to look for or accept the good qualities in everyone. There are some people with truly rotten qualities that have nothing to do with their addiction. Then there are some good people with wonderful qualities who are just not a good match for you. And, there are some whose substance misuse behaviors are absolutely intolerable, in spite of their good qualities when sober or substance free.

Don't take what's said personally. You would not be reading this book if you didn't know the frustration of trying to convince your loved one that his or her drinking/drugging is a problem. You would not be reading this book if you didn't know what it was like to talk to an alcoholic/addict at night and then find out the next morning that your loved one has no recollection of what was said, let alone any agreements that were made.

Understanding that you have been talking to someone whose substance misuse altered the neural networks necessary to "think straight" and act responsibly helps you understand that you have not been talking to the loved one you once knew. Knowing this helps you not to take their substance misuse behaviors personally, or to expect "all is well" during early treatment and recovery.

Understand that conflict is simply a difference of opinion, and a difference of opinion does not have to mean a fight. You don't have to agree with another person's opinion, and s/he does not have to agree with yours. No one has to be "right." This can be extremely hard for family members and friends to do because they see unresolved conflict as a reflection on them – as if it's proof they are somehow the one who is at fault, wrong or not good enough. Therefore, family members and friends tend to argue until the other person agrees with them. But as time goes on, this need to argue becomes a target for the alcoholic/addict to latch on to in their attempt to deflect their addiction/substance misuse or early treatment/recovery behaviors. (Don't forget the code word suggestion mentioned in Chapter 8 as a way to diffuse conflict during a loved one's early treatment and recovery.)

Walk away. If you don't want to talk at that moment because you don't know what to say or are too upset and the other person is pressing you to keep going, walk away. You don't have to stay and fight or talk just because the other person insists on it. Instead, say something like, "I'll have to get back to you on that," and then walk away. Walking away is not "saying" the other person is right. It is simply giving yourself time to collect your thoughts and then say what you want to say when you are ready to say it.

Take people at their word. Try not to attach your emotions, thoughts and feelings to another person's words. When you do, you are reacting to the emotion triggered by what you *think* was said. Instead, take their words at face value. If you really are wondering what they meant, then ask them directly. "It sounds like you are unsure about whether you want me to go out. Did I hear your question correctly?"

Know that NO ONE has to agree with your truth. Think about it – when there is an accident, there can be several witnesses and each one might see the same accident in a slightly different way. This is how we must think about speaking our truth. If it's our truth, then it's what we feel, we see, we want, we need. We do not have to get the other person's agreement or approval in order to make it true for us.

Suggestions to Improve Communication

Don't take offense. The offensive moves (such as deflecting, blaming, excusing, bullying, yelling) that alcoholics/addicts use give them power WHEN YOU REACT to them by going on the defensive and acting on the emotion they've triggered.

For example, when you react to the alcoholic/addict's anger with your own anger or to their denial with accusations or to their broken promises with pleading or a tirade about how rotten they are, you give him/her a target. For when *you* get defensive ("take" offense), *your* reactions and behaviors become their target. In this way, the alcoholic/addict doesn't have to take responsibility for what s/he's done nor wonder what you are thinking nor feel the shame of having let him/herself (and you) down yet again. Instead, s/he can lay it all on you. For example, alcoholics/addicts can tell themselves things like, "Why bother? Nothing I do is good enough." "Who wouldn't drink with someone like you nagging all the time?" "And she says *I* have a problem with anger – ha!"

"Say What You Mean, Mean What You Say and Don't Be Mean When You Say It"

Learning to speak up for yourself – sometimes called "speaking your truth" in the world of addiction treatment – produces amazing results. These results occur not only in dealings with the alcoholic/addict but in your other relationships, as well. It is often hard to do, however, or at least takes practice given how long the unacceptable has been taken as normal. For example, have you ever answered a question such as, "Do you mind if I go out?" with something like, "Well, okay if you *want* to go."

When you think about it, however, what you're really saying (without saying it out loud) is, "Yes, I *do* mind if you go out." And, if the person asking the question took you at your word and left, you would probably be mad because s/he didn't guess what you really wanted him/her to do. But the other person can't read your mind.

In this example, you likely don't trust that you have the right to ask someone to do something for you. Asking doesn't mean you'll get it, but at least you won't be mad about something that may or may not have happened. For example, if you'd answered the question, with, "I'd really like you to stay with me this evening," that's the truth of how you feel. It then gives the person doing the asking the opportunity to either say, "No problem. I'd love to stay here with you." Or "How about if we spend tomorrow evening together. I really would like to go out tonight." Speaking your truth gives you the opportunity to receive another's honest answer.

By the same token, you could be on the flip side of this exchange – the one being asked the question. In that scenario, you might hear the question, "Do you mind if I go out?" as "Please ask me to stay." For listening is the other side of direct communication and speaking your truth. In codependent relationships, codependents become experts at "hearing" their own feelings – the feelings they attach to their emotional reaction to another person's words and that are not necessarily those of the person doing the speaking.

In hearing *your* feelings to spoken words, you are reacting to something that may or may not be true. You are reacting to what you *think* is being said and then adjusting your truth and your responses to accommodate your interpretation, instead of simply taking others at their word.

Taking people at their word and asking for clarification if you're not sure what they meant leaves any further explanation up to them to provide and not for you to second guess.

Realize "No." is a complete sentence. You don't have to explain yourself unless you want to. If pressed to say more, you can say, "No, not now. Please give me some time to think about it." Remember: Respond, don't React. And, remember, too, you have a right to choose *how* and *if* you wish to respond.

Say it only once. It is so easy to say something to a person and when that person doesn't respond in the way you want them to, you then try to use a prodding question or offer a "suggestion," and then a similar, though slightly different suggestion, again, and again, and even a few days later – again. These kinds of efforts are actually attempts to manipulate and/or control another person's thinking so it matches your own. Manipulation is a huge part of "communicating" in the homes of alcoholics/addicts because it's impossible to enforce the "Rules" if one person starts telling the truth.

Suggestions To Help With Setting Boundaries

Only set boundaries you can keep:
- You cannot simultaneously set a boundary and take care of another person's feelings – other people may not like the boundary, but it is one you must set for *you*.

- Do not set a boundary you cannot enforce (for example, if you say, "Drink again, and I'm leaving!" You must be prepared to leave, which means you have taken the time to figure out things like what you'll take, where you'll go and how you'll leave.) If you keep changing the boundaries you set, the alcoholic/addict will know s/he can get you to change your mind the next time. Giving in and then being let down again leaves you angry and frustrated.

Know the "red flags" that indicate it's likely time to set a boundary:
- When you are feeling anxious or ashamed or afraid or angry, it is generally time to set a boundary. That boundary could be just stopping yourself from going further with your reaction until you figure out the real cause or a better response.

- When you find yourself wanting to get someone to do something you think they should do, it's likely you are "focusing over there" to avoid thinking about or addressing what's really bothering you. Try to catch yourself and figure out what's going on. And, it may be that you *do* have a good idea that might help that person – in which case you need to just say, "I have a suggestion, would you like to hear it?"

- When you keep trying to make your point in all sorts of different ways, you are probably trying to control the situation and its outcomes. Instead, set the boundary, say it once and then stop. Don't worry, the other person heard you. And if you say it only once, just think – you're free to do lots of other things!

- When you are complaining or rehashing the same transgression over and over or you keep repeating the same scenario looking for validation of the "rightness" of your part in a situation, it is usually time to set a boundary. Quite possibly the boundary may be for you to apologize for your part in the "conflict."

- When you find yourself feeling defensive or telling "little white lies" to justify your behaviors or thoughts, it's time to remember you don't have to get another's approval for what you think/feel. Set the boundary of stopping yourself until you can sort it out and then speak your truth, and if you owe an apology, go back and make one.

- When you find yourself judging or gossiping, it can be a sign that you are assigning your thoughts and feelings to what someone else has said or done. Or you might be focusing "over there" as a way of assuring yourself that you aren't that bad. In either case, stop and ask yourself, "Is this my business?" And, if it turns out to be a case of assigning your thoughts and feelings to what someone else has said or done, you can go back and clarify what *they* meant and then regroup.

- When you find yourself thinking in polar opposites – all good/all bad – it's likely something has you way out of sorts, but you haven't stopped your thoughts long enough to wade through the muck in order to get at the real issue. Setting the boundary in this situation might simply mean taking some time to think it through.

In closing this chapter, please understand that like addiction treatment, no one size fits all when it comes to helping family members and friends deal with what has happened to them as a result of coping with secondhand drinking/drugging. Start with the four things you can do now to start improving the health of your neural networks: nutrition, exercise, sleep and mindfulness activities. Then take on these other suggestions as you can. You don't (and can't) do all of it at once.

The entire objective is to make changes that feel reasonable and right to *you*. See how those feel. If they help, keep at them and then move forward with another change when *you're* ready. As you incorporate some of these suggestions and as they become your new way of interacting with your alcoholic/addict loved one, these new coping behaviors will spill over into all of your other interpersonal relationships, as well. They will become your new, grooved "thinking" behaviors (as opposed to your old, grooved "reacting" behaviors). Best of all, they will free you to enjoy your life.

Checking Items Off the List

✔ **Learn about the additional tools that can help you whether or not your loved one starts and/or continues treatment and recovery.**

Points to Remember:

- Following the suggestions in this chapter (or coming up with your own) to jar your thinking, change your perspective, improve communication and set boundaries will help you rewire your neural networks and move yourself from reacting (Limbic System) to responding (Cerebral Cortex).

- Just as with addiction treatment, there is no "one size fits all" when it comes to helping a family member or friend who has experienced the effects of chronic secondhand drinking/drugging. It is important to keep in mind that you may or may not be ready to follow any of these suggestions, nor may you particularly need them, depending on your situation.

CHAPTER 13

A Few Final Suggestions – Plus,
What to Say to Children,
Extended Family and Friends

In the families and among the friends of addicts/alcoholics, an odd but common phenomenon takes place: different family members and/or friends can have wildly different recollections of their lives in the same household or their relationship with the same individual. There is often disagreement about what happened or what's happening, how bad it was or is, and who was right and who was wrong. For example, the oldest child may recall mom as a wonderful, loving mother who baked cookies all the time, and the youngest of five might remember her as a "drunk" whose behaviors were so awful, he refused to bring his friends home. These kinds of differing memories can cause family members and friends to argue amongst themselves – all vying for one or the other to see it from their perspective or agree with their recollections and thereby validate their experiences.

It is important to understand that each family member/friend is correct. First of all, each individual sees things from his or her own perspective because of their uniqueness as an individual and their differing personalities. Just remember the courtroom scene where you have two sides telling opposite stories about the "truth" of what happened. That's what can happen in families and among friends.

Secondly, the number of years and the stage at which those years were spent with the actively drinking/drugging alcoholic/addict will also change a person's perspective. Remember, the disease of addiction is progressive. As the alcoholic/ addict's disease progresses, so do their substance misuse behaviors. The way the children recall their time with the non-drinking/drugging parent will differ, as well, for the unhealthy coping skills and behaviors s/he developed also get worse as the disease progresses.

This information can help family members and friends avoid unnecessary arguments when/if they don't all remember "life at home" or "life in the friendship" in the same way.

And, here are a few final suggestions to consider.

105

Anticipate Your Own Slips and Relapses; They're Part of Healing Your Neural Networks

Be neither surprised nor disheartened when you relapse (going full-tilt back to old reactions) or slip (temporarily reverting to old behaviors for a moment). Just like the addict/alcoholic, you are trying to change some deeply grooved, embedded brain maps. And, if your loved one is in treatment, you will experience the impact of the neural network changes that he or she undergoes during the process of treatment and recovery, as well. On top of that, if you have children (who are dealing with their own version of the effects of secondhand drinking/drugging), that adds a whole other layer to the issues you face (and may increase the likelihood of your slipping or relapsing). Try not to get discouraged. It really is worth the effort. It just takes time.

Use your slips and relapses as opportunities for learning, not as reasons to beat yourself up. Unlearning years of the repeatedly activated, reactionary coping skills and behaviors does not happen over night. Knowing some of the signs that a relapse may be lurking can help you take steps to avoid it or minimize its impact. Here are a few of those signs:

Taking on too much. For some codependents, always keeping busy and doing "something" is how they keep their emotions at bay and make the feelings go away. However, taking on more than you can physically and emotionally handle can leave you exhausted. Taking on too much makes clear-headed thinking even more difficult. This then makes reacting and NOT responding more likely. For some, taking on too much also leads to procrastination – the feeling of being overwhelmed by so much to do and not knowing where to start, so you do nothing or something other than the task at hand instead.

White lies and other dishonest behaviors. When you feel the need to cover up or deny your feelings or values by telling yourself, "It's no big deal, it's just a little white lie," it's generally a sign that an old, ineffective behavior is re-emerging.

Argumentativeness/Defensiveness. Picking at others and/or defending yourself for small (in the overall scheme of things) or ridiculous points or behaviors are signs that you are not dealing with a bigger, underlying issue. Trying to defend yourself against the "logic" of an addict/alcoholic who is not in recovery or one who is in early treatment… well, let's just say, there usually can't be much "logic."

Depression. This is not necessarily clinical depression but the sad malaise, "just want to crawl in bed" kind of depression. This often occurs when you are trying to quash your own feelings or desires in deference to another person's. Or it may happen because what is nagging you is "too big" to think through so it feels better not to think at all. Or you may be trying to do far more than humanly possible, given all that is going on with regards to helping yourself and supporting your loved one's recovery. When you get that sad malaise feeling, stop yourself. Make a list. Break it down. Then further break down the list into what is doable today, tomorrow, next week and so on. (Generally, this idea/effort takes practice because it looks so doable on a piece of paper, but when actually trying to fit it in with everything else that "just happens" in a day, it's still too much!) And, by the way, "doable" doesn't necessarily mean taking action. It can also mean setting aside some "thought time" when you can really focus on a problem with no other distractions.

Resentments. There is a saying in the world of addiction treatment, "An expectation is a resentment under construction." Resentments are poison for a family member or friend. They keep us stuck in the emotion, the feeling, whether it is anger, disappointment or feeling sorry for ourselves. To avoid expectations that result in resentments, try to speak your truth – tell the other person what you want or need or are feeling about a given situation. If the other person wants to change or do as you desire, good for you. If they don't, they won't. But, if you don't tell them, they can't. It is the expectation they will do as we desire (or they'll "just know" what we want because they should if they really loved us) that creates the resentment when they don't do what we expected. That resentment, in turn, sets us up to feel sorry for ourselves or to feel like a victim.

Addicts/Alcoholics Will Have Their Own Resentments, As Well

It is not uncommon in early recovery for addicts/alcoholics to forget they have "brain trained" you to expect lying, excuses, broken promises, rationalizations, failure and the like.

Addicts/alcoholics are usually so thrilled (and rightly so) with their sobriety, they expect you to be as thrilled. They may expect you to show it by letting "bygones be bygones" and often act out in hurt or anger when you question where they've been, for example. They forget (or choose not to consider) the reason you question where they've been is because "disappearing acts" generally meant they were using/drinking.

Know that you can and should expect, and deserve, to see a long period of consistent, trustworthy behaviors before you can let down your guard and fully trust again. Addicts/alcoholics need to help you retrain your brain – to help you believe they are where they say they are, doing what they say they'll do and taking responsibility for what they do or don't do. They need to do this by actually "walking the talk," as the saying goes.

When your loved one no longer gives you the vibe (or outright says), "Cut me some slack, I stopped drinking/using, didn't I? And I'm going to meetings and doing everything they tell me to do." – that is when you will know your loved one is "in recovery." And that is what will make you open your heart to trusting, again. Above all, understand that it is not your responsibility to make your loved one's resentments go away.

Other signs of a need for boundaries include gossiping (which means your focus is on someone else's business and not your own); feelings of inordinate anger (likely because you don't know how to cope with the underlying problem) and "yeah, buts." Every time someone (or even you) offers a plausible suggestion to resolve an issue, and in turn, you say, "Yeah, but…," it's likely you are not really listening or being open to the possibility of doing something differently. You are stuck in your old neural network – the one you are trying to change.

When you become aware of one of these signs (gossiping, inordinate anger, "yeah buts"), STOP yourself and think more about what is really going on. You may want to call someone you trust to talk it through or write about it in a journal or take a walk or make a list. Just know you don't have to react immediately or continue reacting. As you calm down and take the time to "reason things out," you can figure out what's really going on, and then you will be able to respond effectively.

Have Some FUN!

Often as we work to come to terms with the consequences of a loved one's substance abuse/addiction, we get so bogged down in trying to get "well" – whether that be by attending meetings, reading recovery books, going to therapy sessions, talking, worrying, struggling against a desperate urgency to start feeling better, NOW – that we miss the opportunities to just have fun.

Fun! It doesn't have to be complicated or take loads of planning. Turn on some music and dance around the house, take a run, join children in *their* world, read a book. "Fun" means we don't talk about any of it, we don't think about it (even if we have to pretend at first). It is a time to completely separate ourselves from all of it and immerse ourselves in the joy of having some fun. Abandoning ourselves for a few moments or 20 minutes or an hour, when we do something that has nothing to do with any of this recovery "stuff," can do us a world of good.

This is especially true when children are involved. Taking time for fun helps everyone start to believe that life really will get better, and trust me, it really does. Recall that recovery for all concerned is about rewiring neural networks, grooving new thought pathways. In this case – grooving pleasure/reward pathways – the ones that rely on dopamine, the neurotransmitter that allows us to experience feelings of happiness and pleasure (and, likely the neural networks that have not been used much, lately!). Having fun is a great way to do this kind of pleasure/reward neural network wiring, and the more you do it, the more grooved those kinds of neural networks will become. Best of all, those are the neural networks that can help you experience happiness and joy by engaging in the simple pleasures available throughout the day.

Talking to Your Children

Often, we assume that because our children have friends, play sports, get along with their teachers, have decent grades and/or work, then all is well with them. But, growing up in an alcoholic/addict family or other dysfunctional-type home deeply affects children.

Recall the discussions earlier in this book about how the brain wires and develops from birth through age 20, often through 25. This helps you understand that growing up in a dysfunctional home (as defined in Chapter 10) exposes children to potentially developing a number of the risk factors – the potential "causes" – for the disease of addiction. These risk factors include social environment, childhood trauma, genetics, mental illness, early use, and of course, substance misuse (described in Chapter 7). This is why it is important to talk with your children about what is (and has been) going on.

Initially, your conversation with your children should be something very simple, along the lines of: "_____ has just been diagnosed with the disease of addiction. This means the way their body and brain handles drugs (or alcohol) makes them say and do things they wouldn't do if they didn't have this disease. _____ is at a place where s/he can get help, so s/he is safe. We are just starting to learn about it, but I want you to understand that I know things have not been "normal" around here. I don't want you to be scared. Just know, I am doing what I can to figure this out, and that _____ can get better."

If your loved one is at a treatment center that offers the services of a family therapist to help the family, then you can ask that person to guide you through this kind of a conversation. If your children start asking questions you can't answer, tell them you don't know the answer but that you are learning as much as you can. Assure them their loved one is safe and things will change.

Then, as you get more certain of your own thoughts and beliefs, sit down with your children to have an open, honest discussion about what has been going on. Let them know what you are doing to make things better for yourself and for them. Allow your children to tell you how awful it has been without interrupting, correcting, dismissing or minimizing what they have to say – even if it's about your behaviors! (And, don't be surprised if they don't know what [or have much] to say in the beginning. They probably don't have words for it, yet.) On your end, this kind of conversation will require:

- an age-appropriate description of alcoholism and/or drug addiction

- a very clear message that addiction is a disease that can be treated – that their loved one can get better and be fun and happy and "normal."

You should have these early conversations with all children present in the beginning, but you should also have one-on-one conversations. Remember, it's not uncommon for each child to have different memories or interpretations of what's happened/happening. As time goes on, initiate new conversations centered on the changes or whatever else they might want to discuss. This is important. It lets your children know they are free to break the crippling rules: Rule #1) drinking/drug use is not the problem, and Rule #2) don't talk about it and attack, minimize or discredit anyone who does.

Above all, try to help your children understand that the disease, not the person inside, is what makes the alcoholic/addict say and do things that are unsettling or scary or weird. You want them to understand that absolutely NOTHING they have done has caused their parent's/sibling's drinking/drugging problems – not their [your children's] fighting, not their bad attitude, not their not showing enough or the right kind of love, not their poor grades, not their messy room – none of it!

And, as you identify and understand your own reactionary behaviors (rage, sadness, silent-treatment), you should also talk to your children about your behaviors and how those may have been unsettling, confusing or scary. You can help your child understand that your reactionary behaviors were all you were capable of at the time because you did not understand substance abuse/addiction and how it affects everyone in the family. In time, help your children look at some of their own coping skills. Getting into fights at school, for example, or arguing with a teacher, may have been the result of their frustrations over their inability to make things better at home. Talking about your unhealthy coping skills will make it okay for them to talk about theirs. Once out in the open, you can decide together what might help them change coping skills they don't like or that get in the way of their success and joy in life.

Try your best not to get negative; not to smear the addict/alcoholic. Remember, it is a disease, and you would want your children to feel free to love their sibling/parent if they had cancer or heart disease.

It might also be helpful to arrange for your children to talk with someone outside the family system, perhaps scheduling a few sessions with a therapist who is trained and experienced in working with children of alcoholics/addicts. Another resource might be a trusted pediatrician. For young people ages 13 and up you might suggest Alateen. The main thrust of all these suggestions is for you to help your children see that it's okay and safe to break the two primary, crippling "Rules."

Above all, you want to assure your child that this disease was something none of you fully understood before and that you are learning a lot of new information. You don't have all of the answers, but you will keep them informed. And, if they have questions, they should be sure to ask you, and you will try to find the answers.

What To Tell Neighbors, Extended Family and Friends

Short answer – only what you are comfortable talking about. You can make it very brief, something along the lines of what you might tell your children early on.

This effort is not about making your neighbors, friends or extended family feel better or forgiving your loved one, nor is it about getting their approval. It is simply a means of letting them know there is a reason for what has happened. Namely, you now understand your loved one has the disease of addiction. There is new, important brain research that explains this, and you are just learning about it. (You might even send them a copy of this book!)

And, One More Thing...

Be patient with yourself. It will take time to unravel the behaviors that were absolutely necessary for you to survive the progression of your loved one's addiction. Here are a few last minute tips:

- Be especially wary of resentments – yours and your loved one's.

- Remember your loved one was incapable of logical thinking. S/he was incapable of understanding any of these kinds of connections: "I drink, I start picking on my wife/husband." "I drink, I get in a fight and go to jail." "I drink, I hurt my children." Instead, his/her thinking was, "I *must* drink, I drink." Thus, every time your loved one promised s/he would stop – tears, pleading and all – s/he meant it. But the neural networks that would have allowed the follow-through on those promises could not override the neural networks that drove every action to the point where the addict/alcoholic had to use their substance again. It will take time and commitment for your loved one to unravel these neural networks.

- Keep your expectations low – not "off" but not a Norman Rockwell family painting, either. Try not to put stock in the hope that *this* will be the holiday you've always dreamed of, for example, because it can't be until a whole lot of recovery happens for all of you. But it will certainly be better than it was before!

- Count to 10 or 100, take a walk, or head to the bathroom and lock the door when it feels as if you'll explode – do anything to break the moment so you can collect your wits about you (and give your neural networks an opportunity to switch from Limbic System reactions to Cerebral Cortex responses). Know this is not to suggest you should stop an emotion or feeling (in fact, it is imperative that you allow yourself to "have" your emotions and feelings), rather it is to buy yourself time to decide on how you want to react to them, if at all.

- If a worry keeps poking into your thoughts, don't run from it. Face it. Even if "facing" it is simply to mark your calendar with a time-period when you can/want to think about and/or take care of the worry. That can be in a day, a week or even a month or two down the line. We don't have to have the answers or solutions immediately, but getting it out of our minds by knowing it's "taken care of" (even if that simply means writing it on the calendar for a later date), frees us to enjoy the moments in our day.

- Enjoy the parts you can. When you aren't so caught up with trying to stop what is beyond your control, you can focus on a child, or on yourself or on your own admiration of the meal you have prepared. Try to be "mindfully" engaged in whatever it is you are doing and focus on that.

Above all, know that you are to be commended for your courage and strength to stay with it and do everything you have done to keep things together. You are not at fault. You had no alternative given you were dealing with something you did not understand. But now that you know what and why it happened and what lies ahead, you can take actions that will allow you to make changes that work for *you*.

Don't rush yourself and do not judge yourself harshly. You will make lots of mistakes and sometimes feel like it will never, ever get better. But, it does. Really. Just do what you can, when you can, because any change, no matter how small, is a step away from the craziness and towards a life that's beyond anything you can presently imagine!

For Further Information

- American Society of Addiction Medicine (ASAM), www.asam.org
- The Addiction Project, produced by HBO in partnership with NIAAA, NIDA and the Robert Wood Johnson Foundation, www.hbo.com/addiction
- National Alliance on Mental Illness (NAMI), www.nami.org
- National Institute on Alcohol Abuse and Alcoholism (NIAAA), www.niaaa.nih.gov
- National Institute on Drug Abuse (NIDA), www.drugabuse.gov
- Substance Abuse & Mental Health Services Administration (SAMHSA), U.S. Department of Health and Human Services, www.samhsa.gov
- World Health Organization (WHO) – Alcohol, http://www.who.int/topics/alcohol_drinking/en/

The bibliography also contains additional information resources.

Checking items off the list…

✔ **Learn why family members and friends may perceive the situation differently and how to talk to your children, extended family and friends about what is going on.**

Points to Remember:

- If you have children, it is very important to start talking to them. Growing up with an addict/alcoholic loved one means they face several of the risk factors for developing the disease of addiction, namely genetics, social environment and childhood trauma. Additionally, it means they have likely wired unhealthy coping skills to deal with the secondhand drinking/drugging and allow them to process the unacceptable as somehow acceptable – networked coping skills they will carry into their other relationships, as well. BUT, they have a huge advantage – they are young and can rewire their brains before the unhealthy networks become too deeply embedded or expose them to further consequences.

- Commend yourself – truly! You have done a Herculean job taking care of everybody's needs so far. Now it is time to take care of yours.

- All of this will take time, but it is absolutely doable, and life really will get better.

Acknowledgements

This book would not have been possible without the stories and conversations shared by and with family members, friends, addicts, alcoholics, clinicians, therapists, professionals, students, teachers – the swath of society so deeply affected by secondhand drinking/drugging, the impacts of a person's substance misuse and/or addiction. These people's experiences, concerns, courage and recovery helped to focus my research and select the questions to answer in order to best help a person faced with a loved one's addiction, treatment and recovery.

I want to thank Catherine Bitler for her help with how to most effectively explain the new brain research and the various other brain-related concepts, as well as the many others who read the manuscript-in-progress and offered their insights, encouragement and suggestions. I want to thank my editor, Mary Claire Blakeman, who, again, helped me with not only her astute editorial suggestions but friendship, as well.

And, I want to thank the scientists, medical professionals and researchers – those on the front lines of the new brain and addiction-related discoveries that are changing how we view and treat addiction and how we can help those who are equally effected – the family members and friends.

About the Author

Lisa Frederiksen has explored a wide-range of topics over the course of her writing, speaking and consulting career, including: civil and women's rights issues, results-oriented workplace initiatives, women's history month celebrations, career search and job hunting techniques, voter empowerment, substance abuse and addictions. The driving force in her work is her desire to understand the various aspects of issues or problems that have either directly affected her life or had significant ramifications on public policy decisions.

Today, Lisa focuses her work in the areas of women's history and alcohol and addiction-related issues, the latter in light of her forty years experience with family alcohol abuse and alcoholism, including seven-plus years of research and recovery. Some of her previous books include: *Freedom Cannot Rest, Ella Baker and the Civil Rights Movement, Women's Rights and Nothing Less, the Story of Elizabeth Cady Stanton, Women's Work, the Story of Betty Friedan* and *If You Loved Me, You'd Stop! What You Really Need To Know When Your Loved One Drinks Too Much*.

Writing, speaking and consulting have not always been Lisa's vocation, however. She earned her Bachelor of Arts degree in Economics from the University of California at Davis and worked during the subsequent twenty-year period in executive management positions. Lisa lives in northern California and enjoys hiking, scuba diving and traveling.

VISIT HER WEBSITE:

www.breakingthecycles.com

Bibliography

"The Addiction Project," Home Box Office, Inc. (HBO) in partnership with the Robert Wood Johnson Foundation, the National Institute on Drug Abuse and the National Institute on Alcohol Abuse and Alcoholism, 2010, <http://www.hbo.com/addiction>

Amen, M.D., Daniel G., Amen Clinics, Inc., <http://www.amenclinics.com/>

American Academy of Pediatrics Committee on Substance Abuse, "Policy Statement Alcohol Use by Youth and Adolescents: A Pediatric Concern," PEDIATRICS®, Official Journal of the American Academy of Pediatrics, April 12, 2010, downloaded from <http://www.pediatrics.org> on May 11, 2010.

American Medical Association, Alcohol and Other Drug Abuse, <http://www.ama-assn.org/ama/pub/physician-resources/public-health/promoting-healthy-lifestyles/alcohol-other-drug-abuse.shtml>

American Public Health Association and Education Development Center, Inc., "Alcohol Screening and Brief Intervention, A Guide for Public Health Practitioners," Washington D.C.,: National Highway Traffic Safety Administration, U.S. Department of Transportation, 2008.

American Society of Addiction Medicine (ASAM), < http://www.asam.org/>

Anderson, Pamela, et al., "Screening & Brief Intervention: Making a Public Difference," Join Together with support from the Robert Wood Johnson Foundation, 2008.

Beattie, Melody, Codependent No More, How To Stop Controlling Others and start Caring For Yourself, Center City, MN: Hazelden®, 1987, Second Edition, 1992.

Begley, Sharon, The Plastic Mind, New Science Reveals Our Extraordinary Potential to Transform Ourselves, London: Constable & Robinson Ltd., 2009.

Black, Claudia, Ph.D., Straight Talk from Claudia Black, What Recovering Parents Should Tell Their Kids About Drugs and Alcohol, Center City, MN: Hazelden, 2003.

Brown, Stephanie and Virginia Lewis, Ph.D., The Alcoholic Family in Recovery, a Developmental Model, New York: The Guilford Press, 1999.

Brown, Stephanie and Virginia Lewis, Ph.D., with Andrew Liotta, The Family Recovery Guide, a Map for Healthy Growth, Oakland: New Harbinger Publications, Inc., 2000.

Carter, Rita, et al., The Human Brain Book, New York: DK (Dorling Kindersley Limited) Publishing, 2009.

Center for Substance Abuse Treatment, "Managing Depressive Symptoms in Substance Abuse Clients During Early Recovery, Treatment Improvement Protocol (TIP) Series 48, DHHS Publication No. (SMA) 08-4353," Rockville, MD: Substance Abuse and Mental Health Services, Administration, 2008.

Committee on Developing a Strategy to Reduce and Prevent Underage Drinking, "Reducing Underage Drinking, a Collective Responsibility," National Research Council Institute of Medicine, Washington, D.C.: The National Academies Press, 2004.

Co-Occurring Center for Excellence, "Treatment, Volume 2: Addressing Co-Occurring Disorders in Non-Traditional Service Settings," U.S. Department of Health and Human Services Substance Abuse and Mental Health Services Administration Center for Mental Health Services, Center for Substance Abuse Treatment, <www.samhsa.gov>, date posted on website: 6/8/06.

Doidge, M.D., Norman, The Brain That Heals Itself, Stories of Personal Triumph from the Frontiers of Brain Science, New York: Penguin Books, 2007.

Doraiswamy, M.D., P. Murali, "Boost Your Brain Health," AARP The Magazine, March/April 2010, pgs. 47-50.

The Franklin Institute Resources for Science Learning, "The Human Brain," The Franklin Institute's Center for Innovation in Science Learning (CISL), <http://www.fi.edu/learn/brain/>

Galanter, M.D., Marc and Herbert D.Kleber, M.D., The American Psychiatric Publishing Textbook of Substance Abuse Treatment, Fourth Edition, Washington, D.C.: American Psychiatric Publishing, Inc., 2008.

Hales, Robert E., M.D., MBA, et al., Study Guide to Substance Abuse Treatment, A Companion to the American Psychiatric Publishing Textbook of Substance Abuse Treatment, Fourth Edition, Washington, D.C.: American Psychiatric Publishing, Inc., 2008.

Ketcham, Katherine and William F., Asbury with Mel Schulstad and Arthur P. Ciaramicoli, Ed.D., PhD., Beyond the Influence, Understanding and Defeating Alcoholism, New York: Bantam Books, 2000.

Kolb, Ph.D, Bryan and Ian Q. Whishaw, Ph.D., An Introduction to Brain and Behavior, Second Edition, New York: Worth Publishers, 2006, 2001.

Kotulak, Ronald, Inside the Brain, Revolutionary Discoveries of How the Mind Works, Kansas City: Andrews McMeel Publishing, 1997.

Le Foll, Bernard and Steven R. Goldberg, "Cannabinoid CB1 Receptor Antagonists and Promising New Medications for Drug Dependence," The Journal of Pharmacology and Experimental Therapeutics, Preclinical Pharmacology Section, Behavioral Neuroscience Research Branch, National Institute on Drug Abuse, National Institutes of Health, Department of Health and Human Services, Baltimore, Maryland, Received September 15, 2004; accepted October 27, 2004.

Mawell, Ruth, Breakthrough, What to Do When Alcoholism or Chemical Dependency Hits Close to Home, New York: Ballantine Books, 1986.

National Alliance on Mental Illness (NAMI), < http://www.nami.org/>

National Association of Social Workers, "Alcoholism and Alcohol Abuse," <http://www.naswdc.org/research/naswresearch/0507alcohol/default.asp>

National Institute on Alcohol Abuse and Alcoholism (NIAAA) of the National Institutes of Health (NIH), < http://www.niaaa.nih.gov/>

National Institute on Drug Abuse (NIDA) of the National Institutes of Health (NIH), < http://www.drugabuse.gov/>

NRTA: AARP's Educator Community and The Dana Alliance for Brain Initiatives, "Staying Sharp, Successful Aging and Your Brain, Current Advances in Brain Research," NRTA and The Dana Alliance, 2009.

NIAAA, "Module 1: Epidemiology of Alcohol Problems in the United States," Updated 2005, <pubs.niaaa.nih.gov/.../Module1Epidemiology/Module1.html>

NIAAA, "Module 10J: Alcohol and the Family," Updated 2005, <pubs.niaaa.nih.gov/publications/.../Module10JFamilies/Module10J.html>

NIAAA, "Statistical Snapshot of Underage Drinking," <www.niaaa.nih.gov/aboutniaaa/niaaasponsoredprograms/statisticalsnapshotunderagedrinking.htm>

NIDA, "Brain Power! The NIDA Junior Scientist Program, "How Drugs Affect the Brain (Module 6), September 19, 2008, <http://www.drugabuse.gov/jsp/jsp.html>

NIH NIDA, "Principles of Drug Addiction Treatment, A Research-Based Guide," NIH U.S. Department of Health and Human Services, NIH Publication No. 09-4180, Second Edition, Revised April 2009.

Office of the Surgeon General, "The Surgeon General's Call to Action To Prevent and Reduce Underage Drinking 2007," U.S. Department of Health and Human Services, Rockville, MD, <http://www.surgeongeneral.gov/topics/underagedrinking/>

Ratey, M.D., John J. with Erick Hagerman, SPARK, the Revolutionary New Science of Exercise and the Brain, New York: Little Brown & Co., 2008.

Ries, M.D., FAPA, FASAM, Richard K., et al. (editors), Principles of Addiction Medicine, Fourth Edition, Philadelphia: Lippincott Williams & Wilkins, 2009.

Ruiz, M.D., Pedro, et al., The Substance Abuse Handbook, Philadelphia: Lippincott Williams & Wilkins, 2007.

Stanford, Ph.D., Mark, "A Response to the New York Times on Drug Treatment," December 29, 2008, <http://www.sccgov.org/SCC/docs/Alcohol%20&%20Drug%20Services, %20Department%20of%20(DEP)/attachments/AResponsetotheNYTimesonDrugTreatment.doc>

Substance Abuse and Mental Health Services Administration (SAMHSA) of the U.S. Department of Health and Human Services, <http://www.samhsa.gov/>

Thompson, Paul, Ph.D., Professor of Neurology, Lab of Neuro Imaging UCLA School of Medicine, <http://www.loni.ucla.edu/~thompson/thompson.html>

Winters, Ken, Ph.D., "A Parent's Guide to the Teen Brain," The Partnership for a Drug-Free America®," <http://www.drugfree.org/TeenBrain/science/index.html>

World Health Organization (WHO), "Alcohol," <http://www.who.int/topics/alcohol_drinking/en/>

World Health Organization, "Resolution WHA, [World Health Assembly] 61.4 - Strategies to Reduce the Harmful Use of Alcohol," 2009, <http://www.who.int/substance_abuse/activities/globalstrategy/en/index.html>

Endnotes

Chapter 1

[1] "NIDA InfoFacts: Understanding Drug Abuse and Addiction," National Institute on Drug Abuse (NIDA) of the National Institutes of Health (NIH), last updated 7.27.09, <http://www.drugabuse.gov/Infofacts/understand.html>

Chapter 2

[2] World Health Organization (WHO), "AUDIT," page 2, <http://whqlibdoc.who.int/hq/2001/WHO_MSDMSB_01.6a.pdf >

[3] World Health Organization (WHO), "AUDIT," pages 17, 19, 20, <http://whqlibdoc.who.int/hq/2001/WHO_MSDMSB_01.6a.pdf>

[4] Anderson, Pamela, et al. *Screening & Brief Intervention: Making a Public Health Difference,"* Join Together with support of the Robert Wood Johnson Foundation, 2008, p. 21.

Chapter 3

[5] Amen, Daniel, M.D., "The Science Behind Brain SPECT Imaging," Amen Clinics, Inc. <http://www.amenclinics.com/clinics/information/the-science-behind-brain-spect-imaging/>

[6] Stanford, Ph.D., Mark, "A Response to the *New York Times* on Drug Treatment," December 29, 2008, <http://www.sccgov.org/SCC/docs/Alcohol%20&%20Drug%20Services,%20Department%20of%20(DEP)/attachments/AResponsetotheNYTimesonDrugTreatment.doc>

[7] "NIDA InfoFacts: Understanding Drug Abuse and Addiction," National Institute on Drug Abuse (NIDA) of the National Institutes of Health (NIH), last updated 7.27.09, <http://www.drugabuse.gov/Infofacts/understand.html>

[8] "An Interview with Kathleen T. Brady, M.D., Ph.D.," HBO in partnership with the Robert Wood Johnson Foundation, the National Institute on Drug Abuse and the National Institute on Alcohol Abuse and Alcoholism, 2010, <http://www.hbo.com/addiction/thefilm/supplemental/621_kathleen_brady.html>

[9] *Ibid.*

[10] Volkow, Nora., M.D., "Challenges and Opportunities in Drug Addiction Research, A Decade After the Decade of the Brain," The DANA Foundation, February 18, 2010, http://www.dana.org/news/cerebrum/detail.aspx?id=25324

Chapter 4

[11] Kolb, Ph.D, Bryan and Ian Q. Whishaw, Ph.D., *An Introduction to Brain and Behavior, Second Edition,* New York: Worth Publishers, 2006, 2001, p. 78.

[12] *Ibid.,* p. 79.

[13] The Franklin Institute Resources for Science Learning, "The Human Brain, Receptors Open Doors," <http://www.fi.edu/learn/brain/>

[14] Ratey, M.D., John J. with Eric Hagerman, *SPARK, The Revolutionary New Science of Exercise and the Brain,* New York: Little, Brown and Company, 2008, p. 36.

[15] Doidge, M.D., Norman, *The Brain That Changes Itself, Stories of Personal Triumph from the Frontiers of Brain Science,* New York: Penguin Books, 2007, p. 63.

[16] *Ibid.,* p. 48.

[17] *Ibid.,* p. xx.

Chapter 5

[18] Amen, M.D., Daniel, "Cool Brain Facts," Amen Clinics, Inc.
<http://www.amenclinics.com/brain-science/cool-brain-science/cool-brain-facts/>

[19] *Ibid.*

[20] Winters, Ken, Ph.D., "A Parent's Guide to the Teen Brain," The Partnership for a Drug-Free America®,
<http://www.drugfree.org/TeenBrain/science/index.html>

[21] Thompson, Paul, Ph.D., "Time-Lapse Imaging Tracks Brain Developing From Ages 5 to 20," NIMH/
UCLA Project, <http://www.loni.ucla.edu/~thompson/DEVEL/PR.html>

[22] Amen, M.D., Daniel, "Cool Brain Facts," Amen Clinics, Inc.
<http://www.amenclinics.com/brain-science/cool-brain-science/cool-brain-facts/>

[23] Winters, Ken, Ph.D., "A Parent's Guide to the Teen Brain," The Partnership for a Drug-Free America®,
<http://www.drugfree.org/TeenBrain/science/index.html>

[24] NIDA, "Drug Abuse and Addiction," National Institute on Drug Abuse (NIDA) of the National Institutes
of Health (NIH), September 17, 2008, <http://www.drugabuse.gov/scienceofaddiction/addiction.html>

[25] *Ibid.*

[26] NIAAA, "Snapshot of Underage Drinking," National Institute on Alcohol Abuse and Alcoholism
(NIAAA) of the National Institutes of Health (NIH), <http://www.niaaa.nih.gov/AboutNIAAA/
NIAAASponsoredPrograms/StatisticalSnapshotUnderageDrinking.htm>

[27] Office of the Surgeon General, "The Surgeon General's Call to Action To Prevent and Reduce Underage
Drinking 2007," U.S. Department of Health and Human Services, Rockville, MD, <http://www.
surgeongeneral.gov/topics/underagedrinking/>

[28] Carter, Rita, et al., *The Human Brain Book,* New York: DK (Dorling Kindersley Limited) Publishing,
2009, p. 69.

[29] Doidge, M.D., Norman, *The Brain That Changes Itself, Stories of Personal Triumph from the Frontiers of
Brain Science,* New York: Penguin Books, 2007, p. xx.

Chapter 6

[30] Volkow, M.D., Nora, "Brain Imaging," Home Box Office, Inc. (HBO) in partnership with the Robert
Wood Johnson Foundation, the National Institute on Drug Abuse and the National Institute on Alcohol
Abuse and Alcoholism, 2010, <http://www.hbo.com/addiction/thefilm/centerpiece/616_segment_5.html>

[31] Volkow, M.D., Nora, "The Hijacked Brain," part of "Addiction and the Brain's Pleasure Pathway:
Beyond Willpower" series, Home Box Office, Inc. (HBO) in partnership with the Robert Wood Johnson
Foundation, the National Institute on Drug Abuse and the National Institute on Alcohol Abuse and
Alcoholism, 2010, <http://www.hbo.com/addiction/understanding_addiction/12_pleasure_pathway.html>

[32] NIDA, "Drugs, Brains and Behavior – The Science of Addiction – Drugs and the Brain," National
Institute on Drug Abuse (NIDA) of the National Institutes of Health (NIH), <http://www.nida.nih.gov/
scienceofaddiction/brain.html>

[33] *Ibid.*

[34] *Ibid.*

[35] Volkow, M.D., Nora, "The Hijacked Brain," part of "Addiction and the Brain's Pleasure Pathway:
Beyond Willpower" series, Home Box Office, Inc. (HBO) in partnership with the Robert Wood Johnson
Foundation, the National Institute on Drug Abuse and the National Institute on Alcohol Abuse and
Alcoholism, 2010, <http://www.hbo.com/addiction/understanding_addiction/12_pleasure_pathway.html>

[36] Riggs, M.D., Paula, "Brain Imaging," Home Box Office, Inc. (HBO) in partnership with the Robert Wood Johnson Foundation, the National Institute on Drug Abuse and the National Institute on Alcohol Abuse and Alcoholism, 2010, <http://www.hbo.com/addiction/thefilm/centerpiece/616_segment_5.html>

[37] NIDA, "Drugs, Brains and Behavior – The Science of Addiction – Drugs and the Brain," National Institute on Drug Abuse (NIDA) of the National Institutes of Health (NIH), <http://www.nida.nih.gov/scienceofaddiction/brain.html>

[38] *Ibid.*

[39] Many of the questions contained in this informal Assessment were contributed to and/or developed while working with partners of Garnet Recovery Group LLC (The Global Addiction Recovery Network) and the Paraiso Clinica De Rehabilitacion to design GARNET's Psychosocial and Family Assessments.

Chapter 7

[40] HBO: Addiction, "Why Do Some People Become Addicted?" Home Box Office, Inc. (HBO) in partnership with the Robert Wood Johnson Foundation, the National Institute on Drug Abuse and the National Institute on Alcohol Abuse and Alcoholism, 2010, <http://www.hbo.com/addiction/understanding_addiction/14_some_people_become_addicted.html>

[41] "Factsheet: Dual Diagnosis," Mental Health America, <http://www.nmha.org/index.cfm?objectid=C7DF9405-1372-4D20-C89D7BD2CD1CA1B9>

[42] "Dual Diagnosis and Integrated Treatment of Mental Illness and Substance Abuse Disorder," National Alliance on Mental Illness, <http://www.nami.org/Content/ContentGroups/Helpline1/Dual_Diagnosis_and_Integrated_Treatment_of_Mental_Illness_and_Substance_Abuse_Disorder.htm>

[43] SAMHSA News, "Underage Drinking Prevention Begins With a Conversation," Substance Abuse and Mental Health Services Administration (SAMHSA) of the U.S. Department of Health and Human Services, <http://www.samhsa.gov/samhsaNewsletter/Volume_18_Number_2/UnderageDrinking.aspx>

[44] NIDA, "Drug Abuse and Addiction," National Institute on Drug Abuse (NIDA) of the National Institutes of Health (NIH), September 17, 2008, <http://www.drugabuse.gov/scienceofaddiction/addiction.html>

[45] "Why Do Some People Become Addicted?," Home Box Office, Inc. (HBO) in partnership with the Robert Wood Johnson Foundation, the National Institute on Drug Abuse and the National Institute on Alcohol Abuse and Alcoholism, 2010, <http://www.hbo.com/addiction/understanding_addiction/14_some_people_become_addicted.html>

[46] NIAAA: "Social Work Education for the Prevention and Treatment of Alcohol Use Disorders, Module 10J, Alcohol and the Family, March 2005, <pubs.niaaa.nih.gov/publications/.../Module10JFamilies/Module10J.html>

[47] NIDA, "Drug Abuse and Addiction," National Institute on Drug Abuse (NIDA) of the National Institutes of Health (NIH), September 17, 2008, <http://www.drugabuse.gov/scienceofaddiction/addiction.html>

[48] Many of the questions contained in this informal Assessment were contributed to and/or developed while working with partners of Garnet Recovery Group LLC (The Global Addiction Recovery Network) and the Paraiso Clinica De Rehabilitacion to design GARNET's Psychosocial and Family Assessments.

Chapter 8

[49] Galanter, M.D., Marc and Herbert D.Kleber, M.D., *The American Psychiatric Publishing Textbook of Substance Abuse Treatment, Fourth Edition,* Washington, D.C.: American Psychiatric Publishing, Inc., 2008, p. 94.

[50] *Ibid.,* p. 95.

[51] Ries, M.D., FAPA, FASAM, Richard K., et al. (editors), *Principles of Addiction Medicine, Fourth Edition,* Philadelphia: Lippincott Williams & Wilkins, 2009, p. 388.

[52] Galanter, M.D., Marc and Herbert D.Kleber, M.D., *The American Psychiatric Publishing Textbook of Substance Abuse Treatment, Fourth Edition,* Washington, D.C.: American Psychiatric Publishing, Inc., 2008, pgs. 95-97.

[53] George Washington University Medical Center, "Ensuring Solutions to Alcohol Problems, Primer 1, Executive Summary, Treating Alcoholism as a Chronic Disease," <http://www.ensuringsolutions.org/resources/resources_show.htm?doc_id=329460&cat_id=989>

[54] Ruiz, M.D., Pedro, et al., *The Substance Abuse Handbook,* Philadelphia: Lippincott Williams & Wilkins, 2007, pgs. 403-404.

[55] Galanter, M.D., Marc and Herbert D.Kleber, M.D., The American Psychiatric Publishing Textbook of Substance Abuse Treatment, Fourth Edition, Washington, D.C.: American Psychiatric Publishing, Inc., 2008, pgs. 97-98.

[56] *Ibid.,* pgs. 98-99.

Chapter 9

[57] Many of the questions contained in this informal Assessment were contributed to and/or developed while working with partners of Garnet Recovery Group LLC (The Global Addiction Recovery Network) and the Paraiso Clinica De Rehabilitacion to design GARNET's Psychosocial and Family Assessments.

[58] Ratey, M.D., John J. with Erick Hagerman, *SPARK, the Revolutionary New Science of Exercise and the Brain,* New York: Little Brown & Co., 2008, p. 59.

[59] *Ibid.,* p. 64.

[60] *Ibid.,* p. 65.

[61] *Ibid.,* p. 63.

[62] *Ibid.*

[63] *Ibid.,* p. 60.

[64] *Ibid.,* p. 67.

[65] Carter, Rita, et al., *The Human Brain Book,* New York: DK (Dorling Kindersley Limited) Publishing, 2009, pgs. 126-27.

[66] *Ibid.,* p. 124.

[67] *Ibid.,* p. 167.

[68] *Ibid.,* p. 127.

[69] *Ibid.,* p. 196.

[70] *Ibid.*

Chapter 10

[71] "Factsheet: Codependency," Mental Health America (formerly known as the National Mental Health Association), <http://www.mentalhealthamerica.net/go/codependency>

[72] *Ibid.*

[73] *Ibid.*

[74] An Informal Codependency Assessment, Series of Questions offered by The Sequoia Center, a Drug and Alcohol Treatment Center in Redwood City, CA. Reprinted with permission.

Chapter 11

[75] "Ratey, M.D., John J. with Eric Hagerman, *SPARK, The Revolutionary New Science of Exercise and the Brain,* New York: Little, Brown and Company, 2008, pgs. 37-8.

[76] *Ibid.*, p. 39.

[77] *Ibid.*

[78] Wolpert, Stuart, "Scientists Learn How What You Eat Affects your Brain – and Those of Your Kids," UCLA News, www.newsroom.ucla.edu, July 9, 2008, <http://newsroom.ucla.edu/portal/ucla/scientists-learn-how-food-affects-52668.aspx>

[79] Carter, Rita, et al., *The Human Brain Book,* New York: DK (Dorling Kindersley Limited) Publishing, 2009, p. 45.

[80] Gilmour, Patricia, "Nurturing Health Brains," Bardstown City Schools Comprehensive School Health, January 4, 2010, <http://bardstownschools.us/health/bloghealth/?p=146>

[81] *Ibid.*

[82] Wolpert, Stuart, "Scientists Learn How What You Eat Affects your Brain – and Those of Your Kids," UCLA News, www.newsroom.ucla.edu, July 9, 2008, <http://newsroom.ucla.edu/portal/ucla/scientists-learn-how-food-affects-52668.aspx>

[83] USDA's Dietary Guidelines, U.S. Department of Health and Human Services and U.S. Department of Agriculture, <http://www.mypyramid.gov/guidelines/>

[84] Wolpert, Stuart, "Scientists Learn How What You Eat Affects your Brain – and Those of Your Kids," UCLA News, www.newsroom.ucla.edu, July 9, 2008, < http://newsroom.ucla.edu/portal/ucla/scientists-learn-how-food-affects-52668.aspx>

[85] Ratey, M.D., John J. with Eric Hagerman, *SPARK, The Revolutionary New Science of Exercise and the Brain,* New York: Little, Brown and Company, 2008, p. 5.

[86] Strauch, Barbara, "Put Your Brain to Work," *AARP Bulletin,* April 1, 2010, <http://www.aarp.org/personal-growth/life-stories/info-04-2010/opinion_put_your_brain_to_work_.html>

[87] Ratey, M.D., John J. with Eric Hagerman, SPARK, *The Revolutionary New Science of Exercise and the Brain,* New York: Little, Brown and Company, 2008, p. 4.

[88] NRTA: AARP's Educator Community and The Dana Alliance for Brain Initiatives, "Staying Sharp, Successful Aging and Your Brain, Current Advances in Brain Research," NRTA and The Dana Alliance, 2009, p. 6.

[89] Carter, Rita, et al., *The Human Brain Book,* New York: DK (Dorling Kindersley Limited) Publishing, 2009, p. 184.

[90] NRTA: AARP's Educator Community and The Dana Alliance for Brain Initiatives, "Staying Sharp, Successful Aging, and Your Brain, Current Advances in Brain Research," NRTA and The Dana Alliance, 2009, p. 19.

[91] Carter, Rita, et al., *The Human Brain Book,* New York: DK (Dorling Kindersley Limited) Publishing, 2009, p. 184.